BUILT TO BEAT

CHAOS

BUILT TO BEAT

CHAOS

Biblical Wisdom for
Leading Yourself and Others

GARY HARPST

WILEY

Published by John Wiley & Sons, Inc., Hoboken, New Jersey.
Published simultaneously in Canada.

For general information on our other products and services or for technical support, please contact our Customer Care Department within the United States at (800) 762-2974, outside the United States at (317) 572-3993 or fax (317) 572-4002.

Wiley also publishes its books in a variety of electronic formats. Some content that appears in print may not be available in electronic formats. For more information about Wiley products, visit our web site at www.wiley.com.

Library of Congress Cataloging-in-Publication Data is Available:

ISBN: 9781394158409 (cloth)
ISBN: 9781394158416 (ePub)
ISBN: 9781394158423 (ePDF)

Cover Design: PAUL McCARTHY
Cover Image: © GETTY IMAGES | WESTEND61

SKY10045410_040423

This book is dedicated to:
The Creator.
By Your will, all things exist.
Who else can answer my questions?

Contents

Acknowledgments

People Who Helped with This Book

Rhonda, my wife and life partner, who has provided much encouragement and a sounding board on endless conversations about the application of biblical truth.

My ABF class, who for many years keeps encouraging me to keep digging deeper into the Bible and its hidden gems.

Jack Ridge and Vernon Strong, partners for forty years creating the experiences related in the book.

Rick, Dave, Corey, Cory, Tyler, Adam. What can I say? Your devotion and creativity inspires me every day.

Tom Dinse, Lia Ottaviano, Cary Hill, Dr. Kathryn Fell, Dr. William Reist, Anthony Hixon, Jim Lange, Eric Buehrer, Dr. Brent Sleisman, Dr. Jay Shannon, Dr. Verneda Bachus, David Tofilon, Jamie Harpst, Jordan Harpst, and Anna Harpst. This group was amazing in the thought they devoted to reviewing the manuscript and answering my unending questions. I really cannot express my thanks deeply enough.

Dan Gonder, Eric Kurjan, the late John Crawford, and the team at Strategic Insight Partners for our client-focused learning partnership.

Richard Narramore and the Wiley team. Richard's persistence in challenging me to write this book was the stimulus to take on this project, and the rest of the team brought it to life.

Dotty DeHart and team at DeHart Agency, Gina Adams and team at Adams Group PR, Gideon and team at PugoDesigns for helping to tell our story.

Introduction

Today's leaders face a perfect storm of chaos. The pace and scope of change has been unprecedented. More has changed in the past few years than in the last fifty combined: staff shortages and rising labor costs, changing attitudes toward work, a focus on gender equity and inclusion, emerging generational differences, rampant burnout, the explosion of technology, changing customer preferences, and supply chain disruptions. Finally, what a person must know to lead the workplace of the future feels overwhelming. And all this upheaval has led to more first-time leaders than ever before being thrown into the fray with little or no training.

We have arrived at the point where every day I hear lament about being held hostage by this invisible force called chaos. As you read on, we are going to challenge you to rethink chaos, leadership, and their relationship.

What if chaos was not some evil force but something a benevolent God gave us for a very good reason? And what if you and every person you know was designed to transform chaos into some purpose of their own choosing? What if that was what leadership is really all about?

The central premise of this book is that your existence is not an accident, and neither is your purpose. Every human is created in the image of God and is designed to win at something—to conquer some part of the chaos around them. The biblical language used is unmistakably strong—"mastery," "dominion," "overcoming," "ruling." You were created to be a victor, not a victim.

It would be a misinterpretation of this premise to assume God's intent is for us to have an easy life. No, His intent is for us to have a *meaningful* life. Struggling and battling chaos is not a means to an end; it is an end unto itself. We are created to be creators, and as we

1

battle chaos and create purposeful order, we grow in the knowledge of self and God, and experience the kind of joy we were designed for.

Bringing order out of chaos applies to building anything—raising the next generation, writing a musical composition, cooking a meal, growing food, and building a business. There are no exceptions; all work is intended to be meaningful.

Never in human history have we faced a greater need for leadership. We need individuals who and organizations that define worthwhile purposes and work together to achieve them. *Built to Beat Chaos* is written to encourage you on this mission.

Part 1 of this book focuses on what effective leaders should *know*. It identifies six key biblical truths about human design and why humans are different than the rest of creation. These differences are the keys to understanding the purpose of leadership, why it is so challenging, and why it is so important.

Part 2 focuses on what effective leaders should *do*. Seven specific recommendations for building a habit-forming system encourages leaders to follow processes necessary to master chaos by aligning people around purpose. History reveals the stark reality that organizations are not good at sustaining success over the long term. This part of the book moves beyond concept to application and presents us with tough choices that test our will.

Part 3 focuses on what leaders should *be*. Effective leadership comes from deep within us and has to facilitate behaviors that allow people to work together toward shared purpose. Just as there are laws of physics that govern the universe, there are laws that govern human interaction. These behaviors are essential to making the best practices in Part 2 come to life and engage people at the heart and mind level.

In Chapter 1, I share some of my 40-year battle with chaos and faith, which has served as the refining fire for distilling these principles.

Onward to Part 1.

PART 1

What Effective Leaders Should Know

Part 1 sets the foundational truths upon which the actions of Part 2 and the character traits of Part 3 depend. They are:

1. Chaos Refines Us
2. You Are Designed to Win
3. All Chaos Is Not Alike
4. Purpose Is Your First Responsibility
5. People Don't Obey the Laws of Physics
6. Order Is Easier to Create Than Keep

By the time you complete Part 1, you will have new insights into your purpose and why leadership is the most rewarding and challenging calling for each of us.

CHAPTER 1

Chaos Refines Us

I have refined you, but not as silver is refined.
Rather, I have refined you in the furnace of suffering.
Isaiah 48:10

Is My Situation Worse?

Is chaos today worse than ever? We are all tempted to think so, but I believe this is the wrong question since every generation faces its own unique chaos. The common characteristic of chaos is that it is ever present for all generations, but its characteristics are unique to the time in which it unfolds.

I doubt those who lived through the plague that killed half the population of Europe or those whose homeland has been bombed into oblivion in a war would say our time is worse.

A better question is, what are you facing now, and how will you overcome it? One health care client I work with has the normal challenges of a highly demanding industry. But because of COVID, they have been stretched to the limit of human endurance in their ability to meet people's needs. They struggle with their own

> The good news is that we have been created for a purpose, and even chaos exists for a purpose. And these two purposes are interrelated.

sickness, exhaustion, and discouragement. For them, overcoming this *particular* chaos is the only question that matters at this moment.

The good news is that we have been created for a purpose, and even chaos exists for a purpose. And these two purposes are interrelated.

For those earlier in your career, this connection is not as easy to see. With the benefit of decades in the business world, I am going to share the parts of my journey that helped me see my purpose and the role of chaos in it.

Let's start with a question I asked myself 40 years ago that kicked off the lifelong adventure that has led to this book.

The Question that Started It All

For as long as I can remember, my life has been a quest to identify and solve problems. Before college, this drive manifested itself in organizing and building things. Born before the microcomputer era, my brother and I were always taking apart go-kart engines and rebuilding them. We grew up on a farm, and there was never any shortage of opportunities for exploration.

In college, I gravitated toward business systems analysis—gathering information and defining solutions. In graduate school, I focused on change management. At the time, I was employed by the university as a systems analyst in the business office.

Like any first-time employee, there was a lot I needed to learn just to do my job. But from a career development perspective, observing how work got done around me was more interesting than my work. How decisions were made, how organizations were structured, people's behavior, the impact of technologies—it was an analyst's dream, a fertile learning environment. The only downside was that I didn't have enough time to digest it all.

After a few years, one human behavior question became central to my observations. The initial version of the question was, "Why do people, including me, say one thing but do another?"

> **Why do people, including me, say one thing but do another?**

> Why did I constantly say to myself I wanted one thing but did something else? It seemed like I had a split personality, and I really didn't like it.

For example, people who were vocal about being overwhelmed with too many projects would continue to take on more. Individuals who recognized they talked too much in meetings would keep talking. Or those who would lose their temper couldn't seem to stop, although declaring loudly they wanted to.

Think about your own New Year's resolutions, and you get the picture.

None of these examples are a big deal. But it was the pervasiveness of this pattern that got my attention. I realized I had the same behavior. Why did I constantly say to myself I wanted one thing but did something else? It seemed like I had a split personality, and I didn't like it.

I didn't realize it at the time, but this kind of human behavior underlies one type of chaos that we will discuss in Chapter 3 called "the chaos within."

After a while, my question broadened from contradictory behavior to a more general question: "Why do humans behave the way they do?" Who knew that trying to answer this question would turn into a lifelong pursuit?

Before exploring how I got the answer to my question, a heads-up regarding worldviews.

Differing Worldviews

> If you are unsure or even wary of a biblical view of leadership, please consider this. The people I learn the most from are those who think differently than I do.

If you are unsure or even wary of a biblical view of leadership, please consider this. The people I learn the most from are those who think differently from me.

I particularly admire people who know what they believe and act on

> ## Most of us can rally around the pursuit of truth. If we are relentless, we will eventually find it.

those beliefs. I don't tell other people what to believe; I simply share what I have learned, hoping it will help people in their pursuit of truth.

Most of us can rally around the pursuit of truth. If we are relentless, we will eventually find it. I enjoy being in the presence of truth seekers!

I hope, regardless of your worldview, that you find in me someone who has devoted a lifetime trying to understand what I believe and act accordingly. It is a journey of trial and error. If that sounds interesting, read on!

Back to the question of human behavior.

Seeking Answers

As I sought answers, I started doing research. I read books on psychology, neuroscience, self-help disciplines, business autobiographies, philosophy, world religions, organizational development—you name it, I read it.

In my reading, I learned that C.S. Lewis noticed this same human behavior issue decades before I did and framed the issue more eloquently. He observed:

> *First, that human beings, all over the earth, have this curious idea that they ought to behave in a certain way, and cannot really get rid of it. Second, that they do not in fact behave that way. They know the Law of Nature; they break it. These facts are the foundation of all clear thinking about ourselves and the universe we live in.*
>
> Lewis, C.S. Mere Christianity
> (C.S. Lewis Signature Classics),
> p. 8. HarperCollins. Kindle Edition.

I was struck by Lewis's opinion that these observations (and the answer to the questions they implied) were the foundation of all clear thinking about everything. A pretty big premise that only fed my pursuit. As a last resort, I turned to the Bible and found explanations that resonated. I grew up in a community where people went to church on Sunday, and though our family attended every week, active faith was not part of our family life. We didn't talk about God, biblical truth, or how to apply it. My parents had a quiet faith but were of the Great Depression generation and were pretty quiet about deeper meaning topics. I had read the Bible in high school, but it seemed fragmented and hard to understand.

This time I was reading with a specific question in mind and saw insights on our purpose, design, and behavior that differed from all the other sources I was reading.

> But in this grand "experiment," a conflict between our desires and reason emerged.

The biblical premise is that God created us to be stewards of the earth and do so in relation to Him and each other. And our design was optimized for that purpose. But in this grand "experiment," a conflict between our desires and reason emerged and created misalignments within ourselves, with each other, and with God. These misalignments are the root of our unpredictable behaviors.

This explanation fits with what I had been observing about myself and others. I had what the Bible calls a "metanoia" experience—a deep spiritual change in heart and mind about who I am and why I am here. From that point forward, the biblical framework became increasingly infused into every aspect of my life.

Science and Beyond

You can think of the Bible as a user's manual explaining why we are here and how we are designed and providing wisdom for life. The Bible states that creation itself reveals the truth about God, so I am a huge fan of scientific discovery, as you will see in later chapters.

But I also recognize there are limits to science. Science can't contribute beyond what can be detected or measured with instruments. For example, science can't answer what happened before the beginning or what love is. The Bible reveals what science cannot: the eternal spiritual dimension of life and the unseen and immeasurable relationship with God and the meaning of life.

This book integrates business and biblical principles for leading yourself and others. And it explores the role of human desire in everything we do and how to manage it. But this book cannot change your desires. I can share principles and insights, but the desire to believe them or apply them comes from within you.

> Human desire is the only thing in the universe that is not subject to the laws of physics.

As we will explore later, human desire is the only thing in the universe that is not subject to the laws of physics. At its deepest level, changing human desire is a spiritual topic best explored in a one-on-one interaction with a trusted spiritual advisor. I advocate an advisor who guides you into the teaching and person of Jesus, but only you can decide to explore that path. (Trust me, there is much good news in that journey should you start. You can visit my website at www.garyharpst.com for more resources.)

Returning to the story, about three years after asking my key question, an interesting choice emerged in a Bible study.

Birth of Our First Business

When I was twenty-nine, I attended a Bible study with two friends. Jack Ridge had been a family friend for over fifteen years and was ten years older than I was. He was a mentor to me on my faith journey. Vernon Strong was a new friend who had just started work at Marathon Oil, where I was already employed.

We met in the winter and enjoyed the fire in Jack's family room. In our study, we had been discussing the idea that if what the Bible said was true, then it should affect what we do 24/7, not just one hour a week while we sat in church.

Jack expressed to Vern and me that one way to exercise your faith to the max was to run your own business. That idea was a new thought to me and was the genesis of our adventure of integrating business and faith.

The three of us started an accounting software business for small and midsized organizations and committed ourselves to operate it by biblical principles. People often ask us what that means—how it affects what we do. The biggest difference for the three of us was how we made decisions and responded to difficulties. Read on for examples.

Decision-making

At 29 years old, I was the CEO of the new company and had zero experience in this kind of role. I was immediately thrust into situations that felt over my head: markets, products, hiring, managing, etc. Early on, these stretch challenges caused me to remember the *why* behind the business and that I was not alone in facing these challenges.

I remember one particular day when I went home so discouraged because of a technical problem that I believed we could not go forward. I walked in the door, sat down, and opened up my Bible, and the first words I saw were, "Behold, I am the LORD, the God of all flesh. Is anything too hard for me?" (Jeremiah 32). That verse became an anchor to my faith as we faced "insurmountable" problems over and over.

This example illustrates one way to integrate faith into business life. When you feel you can't go forward, you draw strength and truth from God, not your emotions.

As CEO, I made routine executive leadership decisions, but we always followed the same model for major strategic questions. The three of us would gather for a day, analyze the questions, and review scripture for principles related to the decision. If we weren't on the same page, we would wait. Never in the history of our partnership have we had a split decision or an argument.

Because our faith and desire to please God were more important than the business itself, we could keep perspective in our decisions and not overreact to fear or pressure. After forty years, this relationship continues as it started.

I am not saying this approach is for everyone. It only works if all the owners are of the same mind and share something more important than the business itself. We realize, from what others have told us, that our situation is unusual and never take it for granted.

Over the next twenty years, we had many opportunities to test our decision-making and faith as we experienced the trials of owning a business. We tasted the chaos of rapid growth. We ran out of cash five times and had a major PR win that grew the business 250% in ninety days. That PR win deserves more explanation.

> ## We made lots of mistakes and were deep in chaos. It took us 18 months to recover from this great PR "win."

Our product was headlined in a *PC Magazine* article. (At the time, *PC Magazine*, before the Internet, was the go-to source for making buying decisions.) That great success broke every process we had. We had to install seventy phone lines to handle call volume. But of course, we didn't have people who knew how to answer questions, so most people were put on hold. We took the most knowledgeable people and made them support managers, which took them off the phones. We made lots of mistakes and were deep in chaos. It took us 18 months to recover from this great PR "win."

That event set up strong growth for the next few years but was just a step in the ongoing journey of overcoming chaos.

"I Will Hate You Until the Day I Die"

Five years later, we had to lay off half our workforce because of my strategy decisions. These people were like family. I still remember the day of having to walk into the meeting room, explain the situation, and tell half of the group that they had to find new jobs. Two aspects of this are challenging. One is the impact it has on all these families, and the other is the weight of knowing that your decisions led to this. It was painful to face these dual truths and keep moving forward.

This occurred at the same time our family was on vacation. My commitment to my family at home and my family at work came to a head. I was on the phone late at night trying to keep things on track at the office and playing with my kids during the day.

You've likely experienced how it feels to be stretched in many directions. Rhonda, my wife, gave me her full support in this balancing act, trying to accommodate my schedule and be encouraging in her attitude instead of resentful. Our faith was stronger than our problems, which is a key to sanity when battling chaos.

I don't wish the layoff experience on anyone, but out of it were forged some of my deepest leadership convictions. First, I realized I do not have the role of God in anyone's life. He is the provider for people and not me. This belief helped me process the risk vs. reward of being in business.

Truly, this layoff was painful in the impact it had on people. It sobered me and made me resolve to learn from my mistakes. But it did not destroy me. The faith of the founders and the belief that God is in control, not us, allowed us to go forward.

We realized we couldn't have it both ways. If we wanted the upside of building a business and providing employment, we had to take the downside risk of making mistakes. These kinds of trials by fire force digging deeper about what you believe, which in turn guides your decisions.

My second faith lesson was the realization that I cannot control how other people react. Again, I am not God. I make mistakes. Some people react with bitterness, and some see the bigger picture of God at work.

A couple of years after the layoffs, I received two letters that I keep in my "perspectives" file in my office. One person thanked me for the opportunity to work with us and how the layoffs led her to do something she had always dreamed of: becoming a nurse. She saw God's hand in the whole process.

The other letter was from someone who wanted me to know they would "hate me until the day they died." The chaos that the layoff caused in their life was still controlling them.

I was helped by understanding who I am, who God is, and knowing the difference. This truth allows me to set the right expectations for myself and others.

After the layoffs, our direction changed radically.

Another Lesson: Embrace Constraints

At this point, we had lost a lot of great talent, but what needed to be done was clear. The technology world was rapidly shifting from character-based applications to graphical user interface applications, which in the business world meant Microsoft Windows.

We needed to build a next-generation Windows product and had very few resources to do it. We formed a small team of six people and gave them what seemed like an impossible task: build a new product and have it done in two years.

We had competitors a year ahead of us and large development teams of 100 people reportedly working toward this same objective. But we did not give in to the fear that could have paralyzed us.

> This project resulted in one of my life's most powerful lessons: the value of facing and accepting constraints

This project resulted in one of my life's most powerful lessons: the value of facing and accepting constraints. Because this team had such "ridiculous" constraints, few resources, and a tight schedule, they had to be creative. They realized they could never build an app that quickly from scratch, so they focused on finding existing components and assembling a system out of prebuilt pieces.

The result was stunning to us and our competitors. We launched our new product ahead of almost all of our competitors, which set us on an amazing growth path and led to more decisions, learning, and new kinds of chaos.

Go Public or Sell

Over the next few years, we grew 600% and expanded our partner network to over a thousand, with fifty thousand clients in twenty countries. This high-growth ecosystem became a laboratory for seeing how growth affected the thousands of organizations we interacted with.

And the growth brought us to another big decision.

After twenty years, we were the only privately held company among our major competitors in the US. The rest were publicly traded and had access to more capital to grow their businesses. We were at a crossroads of needing to either merge with a public company or become publicly traded ourselves.

We reached out to two competitors to see if there was interest in a merger. We decided *not* to reach out to Great Plains, our closest competitor in the US, which turned out to be ironic as you will learn.

We found strong interest and went through due diligence with a European company that wanted to build market share in the US. In this process, if the parties get close enough to a deal, they agree in good faith not to enter negotiations with anyone else until a formal term sheet is signed or the negotiation ends.

The term sheet is important because until you have it in writing, everything is subject to change. Most deals that get to the term sheet stage eventually close.

There was one particular week in this process that proved pivotal. It felt chaotic to me. On Monday, our European suiter promised to provide the term sheet on the upcoming Thursday.

On Tuesday, Doug Burgum, CEO of Great Plains, heard the rumors and called to ask if we would consider them in this process. I told him it was too late, but I would let him know if anything changed.

On Thursday, the term sheet did not arrive. I called to find out why and was told that they would not deliver it until the following Monday. This was a major break in trust.

We discussed it and I contacted Doug Burgum to open up the process to Great Plains. I explained it was probably too late for them to catch up, but if they wanted to be considered, we would need a term sheet by Monday, just four days away.

We sent them basic due diligence information, and they got us a term sheet on Saturday—48 hours later! We were impressed with Doug's leadership and ability to move this quickly. And based on past interactions, we knew they were a high-integrity, people-centered organization.

Following our usual decision process of prayer, I signed the term sheet, and we set a closing date for a few weeks later. Again, it may not be obvious, but our faith guided us in this decision.

But wait, there is more chaos to come.

Timing Is Everything

For tax reasons, the transaction was structured as 80% stock and 20% cash, and the cash had to be no more than 20% of the value of the deal. Since the term sheet specifies a price several weeks ahead of closing, no one knows what the stock price will be at closing. So the price is expressed in terms of a fixed amount of cash and a certain number of shares.

We signed the term sheet in March 2000, right at the peak price of the NASDAQ index when Great Plains stock was trading in the 50s. A couple of days before the closing date, Great Plains stock dropped suddenly by over 40% for what we believed were short-term reasons.

This dramatically lowered the price of the deal and created a sudden question of whether to go forward. But Jack, Vern, and I were confident in our decision process and believed Great Plains was the right partner and that this was a temporary pricing issue.

We proceeded with the closing. Not everyone internally agreed with us. But our prayerful decision process anchored our confidence to proceed.

It turns out this sudden drop was quite beneficial to Solomon employees and shareholders. Because the number of deal shares had to be adjusted to ensure the cash portion stayed below 20%, we got more shares at a lower price. As Warren Buffet is fond of saying, "Buy good stocks when they are on sale." Also, all our employee stock options were converted to Great Plains stock at a lower strike price, which meant much higher value when prices returned to normal.

Under Doug Burgum's leadership, the combined company was in good hands. Doug Burgum had a strong relationship with Microsoft, and the combination of our two companies made Great Plains an acquisition opportunity for Microsoft. Within six months, there was a term sheet with Microsoft. And Great Plains stock rebounded in anticipation of the sale to Microsoft.

The net effect financially was that Solomon shareholders had a much better economic result than we would have had if there had not been a sudden drop in price at closing. This is another leadership principle: seek to do the right thing for the right reasons, work with people you trust, pray a lot, and move forward.

Doug joined Microsoft to lead this business unit until his departure several years later. He has since become governor of North Dakota. I decided I didn't want to be a part of that large of an organization and started thinking about what was next. Being a compulsive organizer, I started interfering in my wife's domain at home, and within two weeks, she clarified I needed to find something else to do.

In 2001, I started a company to research how to help organizations manage the chaos associated with growth. After twenty years at Solomon Software and working with hundreds of organizations, this felt like what I was created for. I was now thinking full time about the answer to the questions that started this journey twenty-five years earlier. It has been and still is an adventure!

> It didn't mean trying to coerce people to believe what we did. It meant being truthful, prayerful about decisions, and thinking deeply about why we were doing what we were doing.

What I learned about applying biblical principles in my first twenty years as a CEO may not seem that significant to someone who didn't experience it. It didn't mean trying to coerce people to believe what we did. It did mean being truthful, prayerful about decisions, and thinking deeply about why we were doing what

> Keeping someone in a position they are not good at is the same as lying to them.

we were doing. It meant staying the course even when the going got tough, and it meant routine things such as paying the bills on time. Sometimes it even meant having to fire someone who was not a fit for the job. Keeping someone in a position they are not good at is the same as lying to them. They will never find their place in life if you don't constructively encourage them to move out of the wrong job to find the right one.

As I moved into this next phase of my career, I could reflect on the chaos we experienced in our first twenty years and saw what God had to say about chaos in the Bible.

The First Chaos Was Good

Chaos has been around for a long time. And it is not always a bad thing. The first two sentences of the Bible state: "In the beginning,

Said another way, God's first act was to create some chaos.

"God created the heavens and the earth. The earth was without form and void, and darkness was over the face of the deep" (Genesis 1:1–2).

For reasons not stated, God first created the matter that became the earth in a chaotic state. Said another way, God's first act was to create some chaos. He then transformed that chaos into the earth as we know it. The transformation occurred in the following stages:

- Creation of light in contrast to darkness;
- Separating the water above (clouds) from the water below (oceans);
- Separating the land from the seas;
- Exposing the sun and moon to mark time;
- Adding living creatures to the water and sky;
- Animals added to land, including humankind.

The creation narrative illustrates that chaos is an input to the creative process. As Jok Church says:

Chaos does not mean total disorder. Chaos means a multiplicity of possibilities. Chaos is from the ancient Greek word...and it was about that which is possible, not about the disorder.

https://www.azquotes.com/quote/1024872

Chaos is not only a "raw material." Transforming it is a means of refining us. As I think about my journey so far, it seems the experience is like forging steel.

From Iron Ore to Steel

Forging steel starts with iron ore, which is filled with impurities. That ore is heated to high temperatures to melt off impurities. With the addition of a few key ingredients, it becomes steel.

Drawing an analogy to business, the iron ore is the equivalent of the opportunities in business that you face every day. The heat is the stress of having problems you don't know how to solve, and the key ingredients are biblical principles that don't change no matter how much chaos there is.

> God created chaos in the first place: to challenge us to the deepest level, to burn off the impurities of false hopes and beliefs.

In this extreme "heat," I came to understand biblical truths more deeply than would be possible otherwise. I believe this is the reason God created chaos in the first place: to challenge us to the deepest level, to burn off the impurities of false hopes and beliefs. The result is a character of "steel," which is much more resilient than the iron ore it came from. This process of refining is what the Bible version at the beginning of this chapter is referring to.

I have refined you, but not as silver is refined. Rather,
I have refined you in the furnace of suffering.

Isaiah 48:10

As I reflect on what I have learned about leadership, the outline for this book emerged.

In Chapter 2, we will move on to surprising insights into every person's purpose and how God designed you to fulfill yours.

Takeaways

- Chaos has been around since the beginning, so everyone has to deal with it.
- Chaos was created for a purpose, and so were you. There is a connection (more later).
- Biblical principles change your perspective in decision-making as to what you control and don't.

- People with different worldviews can learn from each other.
- The Bible embraces science and claims that creation reveals the Creator.
- Chaos refines human character and understanding. It tests what you believe.

CHAPTER 2

You Are Designed to Win

Then God said, "Let us make man (humanity) in our image, after our likeness. And let them have dominion over the fish of the sea and over the birds of the heavens and over the livestock and over all the earth and over every creeping thing that creeps on the earth.

Genesis 1

The Craftsperson and Their Chair

As I write this, I am sitting in a handcrafted Stickley chair. (For those who have never heard of Stickley, it is a fourth-generation firm out of New York that builds furniture the old-fashioned way, one piece at a time.) If I were to ask the artisan the purpose of their chairs, I might get a variety of answers:

- A comfortable place for people to sit;
- A keepsake for generations to hand down;
- To make a living;
- The joy of creating them.

These four answers fall into two categories: the first two state requirements for the chair, and the second two are requirements for the craftsperson. Note that the requirements are very different depending on which perspective you use.

In this chapter, we will drill into the requirements for humans (the chair) as stated in the creation narrative. And we also explore how these requirements were satisfied in the design of humans.

In the engineering world, "requirements" state what you want to accomplish, and "design" tells you how to meet the requirements. The Bible gives us insight into the requirements and design of God's "humanity project."

Human Design Requirements

The first premise of the Bible is that humans were designed (by God). And the purpose of humans is answered in 48 words on the first page of the Bible.

Then God said, "Let us make man in our image, after our likeness. And let them have dominion (over the earth)."

The answer is surprising in that the Creator created us to be creators. Note first that the "craftsman" (God) did not make a "chair," He instead created another, more limited version of Himself (another creator).

The assertion that we are created in God's image

raises questions about what that means. To answer that question, we start with what we know about God from the creation narrative. Perhaps learning something about God will teach us something about ourselves.

First, notice that God has a mind. He thinks before He acts. In the first sentence above, He states his intention to create *before* He actually creates. We, too, can think about what we are going to do before we do it.

Next, in the first two sentences of the creation story that follows, God creates the earth in a formless (chaotic) state as His first act.

> *In the beginning, God created the heavens and the earth. The earth was without form and void, and darkness was over the face of the deep.*
>
> Genesis 1

The rest of the chapter 1 creation narrative explains how God progressively brought order to that chaos by separating land from water, light from dark, etc.

His example of bringing order out of chaos provides insight into what God means when He says that we are to have "dominion." *Dominion* means to take responsibility for managing creation—the natural world around us, the birds of the air, the fish of the sea, and the animals of the ground.

Dominion includes a broad range of activities that involve having a purpose and using the surrounding resources to fulfill that purpose. My ancestors prepared swamp land for farming by removing trees and digging drainage ditches. That is dominion. Building a business, raising a family, and cooking a meal are all forms of dominion.

You were created by God to have dominion.

Unfortunately, history is full of people abusing their dominion. This is where the word *dominion* comes to mean "dominate by power or force," and it is condemned in the Bible. The standard in the Bible for leadership is integrity, justice, and righteousness.

The bottom line is that God created us, in His image, not to be ruled by the chaos around us but to rule over it, just as He did

> The bottom line is that God created us, in His image, not to be ruled by the chaos around us but to rule over it.

in the creation narrative. We don't have the same power, but we have been given our own small realm in the universe to rule over.

Next, God clarified that there is power in numbers. Let's look at what that means in our daily lives.

The Multiplication Paradox

The structure of the language in the preceding creation narrative is unusual because it tells us what God is thinking *before* He acts ("Let us make man").

The verse that follows narrates the actual creation of humanity and gives us more information. It is worded in the past tense, indicating He followed through on His thoughts.

> *So God created man in his own image, in the image of God he created him; male and female, he created them. And God blessed them. And God said to them, "Be fruitful and multiply and fill the earth and subdue it and have dominion over the fish of the sea and over the birds of the heavens and over every living thing that moves on the earth."*

> God is clarifying that the only way humanity can fulfill its purpose of ruling over the whole earth is to multiply and "fill it."

He declares His image is expressed, somehow *jointly,* as male and female. This implies the equality of men and women. He also commands them to multiply, implying that it is necessary for dominion. God is clarifying that the only way humanity can fulfill its purpose of ruling over the whole earth is to multiply and "fill it."

This gives us insight into why we are so fixated on sex and family. We are created to do so, and the resulting drive is evidence. We don't just want these things; we need them.

The topic of multiplication has deep implications for leadership. It means that we cannot fulfill our purpose by ourselves.

> This is the first hint that leadership is difficult. In the early years of our family of five, we could not even agree on where to go for dinner.

We have to work with others to do it. Did you ever notice people have problems getting along? This is the first hint that leadership is difficult. In the early years of our family of five, we could not even agree on where to go for dinner.

The Bible is explicit about this paradox, and leaders are caught right in the middle of it. In Chapter 5 we will explore it further.

So far, however, the creation narrative has not provided information about our design. *How* are we equipped to have dominion? For more information on that, we have to fast-forward in the Bible narrative 10 long generations to the time of Noah.

The Creator's Critique

Before digging into our design, one clarification about reading the Bible. It was written to help us understand things above our pay grade. I think an analogy for us trying to understand our design and purpose without the Bible would be like a physicist trying to explain quantum theory to a fly or sex to a two-year-old.

To help our understanding, God uses stories, analogies, and nature to speak to us. I believe the Bible conveys fundamental truth, but we can sometimes miss the point of what it is saying by misinterpreting it.

We pick up our story ten generations after creation. At the scene is God evaluating how His "humanity project" is going in the time of Noah.

As an aside, this story illustrates another way we are like God. When we work to build something, our first instinct is to try it out to see if it works. Did our dream come true? Or do we need to make adjustments?

The scene opens as God observes the situation on earth and shares His thoughts:

The LORD saw that the wickedness of man (humanity) was great on the earth and that every intention of the thoughts of his heart was only evil continually.
And the LORD was sorry that he had made man on the earth, and it grieved him to his heart.
So, the LORD said, "I will blot out man whom I have created from the face of the land, man and animals and creeping things and birds of the heavens, for I am sorry that I have made them."
Genesis 6

First, we see what He observed. Next, we understand His feelings about what He observed, and third, we learn what He will do about it.

There is more to discuss in these three sentences than we can cover in one chapter, so for the rest of this chapter, we will focus on the last half of the first sentence in the preceding extract.

Setting aside how unhappy He is, we are fortunate that in His diagnosis, He reveals some key information about how we are designed. Internalizing this information will help you become a better leader—of yourself and others.

> He reveals that humans have a heart, thoughts, and intentions that lead to action.

The last half of the first sentence states that "every *intention* of the *thoughts* of his (humanity's) *heart* was only evil continually." In this statement, God reveals something *not* revealed in the creation narrative.

He reveals that humans have a heart, thoughts, and intentions that lead to action (implied). We will discuss what He means by *evil* in Chapter 4. For now, we want to probe the relationship among heart, mind, intention, and action.

Let's start with the heart.

Desire Precedes Thought

The first element of our God-created architecture is a "desire engine." It is the place where our "wants" (purpose) originate. The metaphor used to represent that engine is the "heart." (See Figure 2.1.)

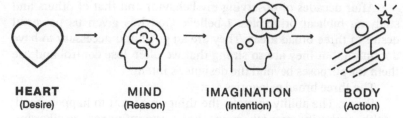

HEART   **MIND**   **IMAGINATION**   **BODY**
(Desire)   (Reason)   (Intention)   (Action)

FIGURE 2.1 The role of desire.

In this narrative, God points to the heart, where the problems start.

In biblical language the heart is in the center of our bodies and represents where desire originates deep within us. In this narrative, God points to the heart where the problems start. It says: "The intentions of the thoughts of the heart were only evil always."

The heart is one of the most frequently referenced topics in the Bible, with over 800 references. The samplings below show how critical the heart is in God's design for humankind.

- "Keep your heart with all vigilance, for from it flow the springs of life" (Proverbs 4:23).
- "You say, 'How I hated discipline, and my heart despised reproof (correction)!'" (Proverbs 5:12).
- "The wise of heart will receive commandments, but a babbling fool will come to ruin" (Proverbs 10:8).
- "Anxiety in a man's heart weighs him down, but a good word makes him glad" (Proverbs 12:25).
- "A tranquil heart gives life to the flesh, but envy makes the bones rot" (Proverbs 14:30).

A theme repeated throughout this book is that being an effective leader requires being a student of desire.

A theme repeated throughout this book is that being an effective leader requires being a student of desire. Deep down, what is it you want? Those around you want?

After decades of observing my behavior and that of others and studying biblical principles, I believe God has given us powerful desire in three broad areas. They are all good and necessary to have dominion, but they are so strong that we often lose control and use them for purposes beyond the designer's intent.

The three broad categories are:

Power. The ability to make the things we want to happen. Skill, wealth, authority, strength, connections, and influence are all examples of power.

Reproduction. It is broader than sex. It includes family, belonging, and community. We all know how strong this desire can be.

Identity. Knowing who I am, why I am here, and where I came from. This is necessary to determine our purpose. Without purpose we cannot overcome chaos. This desire exists to lead us into a relationship with the Creator.

The problem with the word *desire* is that it is not strong enough. *These drives go beyond wants; they are "needs" built into our design. They shape our lives and have expression in what we do in ways and times we don't expect.*

> These drives go beyond wants; they are "needs" built into our design. They shape our lives and have expression in what we do in ways and times we don't expect.

You will be a better leader if you understand the power and presence of desire in everyone you interact with. Engaging the hearts and minds of those around you depends on helping people fulfill these needs. This applies to all of life, not just paid employment.

For example, have you ever noticed a grandmother's passion for preparing Thanksgiving dinner? This is a supreme example of bringing order out of chaos, and you better not get in her way.

Think of the passion of a father protecting a child, a musician performing, or a gardener gardening. We know immediately when we see someone "on a mission."

But what happens when a strong desire is denied? Let's explore a few insights from the Bible.

Desire Denied

Much of the chaos we face in leadership roles originates in the "illogical" things we and others do. This is not a new idea. One example is God confronting people with their illogic by speaking through the prophet Isaiah.

In this situation, some people have a strong desire to worship something. It is so strong that God points out the insanity of how they pursue that desire. They take wood and use half of it for cooking their meal and the other half to make an idol that they bow down to and worship as God.

> Over the half he eats meat; he roasts it and is satisfied. Also he warms himself and says, "Aha, I am warm, I have seen the fire!"
> [17]And the rest of it he makes into a god, his idol, and falls down to it and worships it. He prays to it and says, "Deliver me, for you are my god!"
>
> Isaiah 44

> Reading this passage makes me smile because I see how much easier it is to see the insanity of other people's actions than in my own.

Reading this passage makes me smile because I see how much easier it is to see the insanity of other people's actions than in my own.

As a leader, when trying to sort out the chaos of human interactions, we are more effective when we try to get to the root of what motivates people. Often, the people involved benefit from bringing their underlying desires to the surface because sometimes they (we) are unaware of their effect on our actions.

It is good to be alert for issues of the "heart." Desire can drive us to lose all reason. The Bible warns of several such expressions.

Anger

The first example in scripture is Cain killing his brother, Abel, because God considered Abel's offering better than Cain's. Cain desired God's approval and acceptance and didn't get it. His reaction was anger, which resulted in him murdering Abel. Why? Because Abel had what Cain wanted, the approval by God of his offering.

> *In the course of time, Cain brought to the LORD an offering of the fruit of the ground, and Abel also brought of the first-born of his flock and of their fat portions. And the LORD had regard for Abel and his offering, but for Cain and his offering he had no regard.*
>
> *So Cain was very angry, and his face fell. The LORD said to Cain, "Why are you angry, and why has your face fallen? If you do well, will you not be accepted? And if you do not do well, sin is crouching at the door. Its desire is for you, but you must rule over it."⁸ Cain spoke to Abel, his brother. And when they were in the field, Cain rose up against his brother Abel and killed him.*
>
> Genesis 4:3.

This is another example of how desire overcomes reason. How does killing Abel get Cain what he wants, which is God's approval? Cain offends God even more by killing Abel, which is the opposite of what he wants.

We have other reactions besides anger, however. Sometimes we become afraid.

Fear

Israelites were on a major road trip from Egypt to their homeland. They were almost there and sent spies into a land God had promised them. They hoped to be done traveling.

However, the spies returned to report that the land was extraordinary (filled with milk and honey), *but* powerful people lived there (giants). They would have to fight for what they wanted. The Bible records that their "hearts melted." They lost the will to go forward.

> ³¹*Then the men who had gone up with him said, "We are not able to go up against the people, for they are stronger than we*

are."[32] *So they brought to the people of Israel a bad report of the land that they had spied out, saying, "The land, through which we have gone to spy it out, is a land that devours its inhabitants, and all the people that we saw in it are of great height.*[33] *And there we saw the Nephilim (the sons of Anak, who come from the Nephilim), and we seemed to ourselves like grasshoppers, and so we seemed to them.*

Numbers 13

Fear ultimately led to that generation losing the opportunity to enter its homeland.

A different response from fear is discouragement. This is what the Bible refers to as "heart sick."

Heart Sick

This could lead to a desire for a different type of work, to start a business, or to end their loneliness. Despair can be difficult to detect since it can grow slowly over an extended time, and people mask it. Taken to an extreme, discouragement can evolve to escape into alcohol, drugs, or even suicide.

Hope deferred makes the heart sick, but a desire fulfilled is a tree of life.

Proverbs 13:12

Whereas those who are heart sick are often quiet, there is also an opposite reaction: a variation of anger.

Disruption and Discord

This leads to striking out at others. Typical behaviors include outbursts, uncooperativeness, and doing things that make it difficult for people to work together, all of which lead to chaos.

These people appear unhappy and work at making everyone else unhappy, too. The Apostle James found this behavior in the church as well. Wherever there are people, there are clashes of desire.

What causes quarrels and what causes fights among you? Is it not this, that your passions are at war within you? You desire and do not have, so you murder. You covet and cannot obtain, so you fight and quarrel.

James 4

To illustrate, I consulted on a situation in a nonprofit with several hundred people employed. One individual started disrupting an entire department after years of good work. It took digging, but the cause was that his wife told him that someone in the group had made a suggestive remark to her.

He told no one; he just took out his frustration and anger on everyone else. I arranged a conversation between this man and the alleged offender, and the other party denied it. Their interaction damaged their relationship beyond repair and affected the entire team. Resolution did not occur until one party left the organization for another job.

> My first reaction when I see someone behaving like this is to get angry at them. But a more constructive thing to do is find out the reasons behind the emotion.

My first reaction when I see someone behaving like this is to get angry at them. But a more constructive thing to do is find out the reasons behind the emotion. Then we can work on the root problem rather than adding to the problem with our own unpredictable reactions.

Envy

Envy is resentment toward someone who has what you want. This can grow into the extreme of not only wanting something for yourself but also *not* wanting someone else to have it. (Think Cain.)

Scripture illustrates this principle with a story where King Solomon had to discern between two women who claimed the same baby as their own. Solomon said to bring a sword to cut the baby in two, so each woman could have half.

> Desire is like nitroglycerin. Handle with care. We all have had our desires trample our reason.

As a wise leader, he understood the actual mother desired life for her baby ahead of not wanting someone else to have it. The false mother, in contrast, revealed herself because of her envious response. She was willing to see the baby die rather than allow the other woman to have it.

Envy is another extreme example that leads to a word of caution. Desire is like nitroglycerin. Handle with care. We all have had our desires trample our reason. As leaders, we need to be better at helping people trapped in this situation. We should be more understanding since we've all been there.

Chapter 14 focuses on this topic. This chapter aims to build awareness of the power of desire—both constructive and destructive. The Bible makes clear why desire is so strong in us; we need it to overcome chaos and have dominion.

Let's move on to how our minds interact with our desires.

Thought Precedes Intention

As God muses on the condition of His creation, He references "thoughts." The Hebrew root word means to "weave" or "fabricate." It conveys the idea of building something in your mind. (See Figure 2.2.)

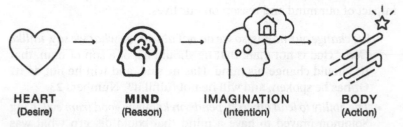

| HEART | MIND | IMAGINATION | BODY |
| (Desire) | (Reason) | (Intention) | (Action) |

FIGURE 2.2 The role of reason.

Thoughts can be confusing and conflicting while you are sorting through options. Lack of experience and knowledge limits our thinking. Thinking is a messy, hard-to-explain process. Hopefully, after enough thinking, its "output" is a mental picture—an intention emerges.

Bouncing ideas off others and talking things through aids the thought process. Like actions, thoughts can be constructive ("good") or destructive ("evil"). Good thoughts are based on truth and lead to action that aligns with enduring principles. Evil thoughts lead to actions that result in the breakdown (decay) of good things. In the next chapter, we will drill into the surprising meaning of *good* and *evil*.

Sometimes we (I) move straight from desire to action. We react to something so quickly that we do not think. Sometimes the consequences are immediate, and other times the results don't emerge for an extended period.

> A significant distinction between humans and animals is our ability to filter our desires through the lens of reason.

A significant distinction between humans and animals is our ability to filter our desires through the lens of reason. For example, let's say that I get an important text while driving. Will reading it lead to good things or not? Humans can use reason to think about the consequences of such an action.

Animals, alternatively, have a tiny filter for their actions. If a male dog sees a female dog in heat, it isn't long before he acts on his desires with no complications about what is right or wrong.

The Bible has hundreds of references to the mind and how it functions. Following are a few wide-ranging observations about the human mind. I include them to show the Bible's emphasis on the impact of our mind and reason on our lives.

- *We change our minds, so we do not always do what we say, unlike God.* "God is not man, that he should lie, or a son of man, that he should change his mind. Has he said, and will he not do it? Or has he spoken, and will he not fulfill it?" Numbers 23
- *The ability to lead others depends on knowing good from evil.* King Solomon prayed to have a mind that could discern what was right and wrong. He knew he could not be a good leader without that ability. "Give your servant, therefore, an understanding

mind to govern your people, that I may discern between good and evil, for who can govern this, your great people?" Kings 3:9

- *Our plans don't override God's.* "Many are the plans in the mind of a man, but it is the purpose of the LORD that will stand." Proverbs 19:21

- *We should not trust our minds in isolation.* We easily lose perspective, jump to conclusions, or lack the experience to evaluate all the factors required for a good decision. Self-awareness of our limitations is part of what the Bible calls wisdom. "Whoever trusts in his own mind is a fool, but it will deliver him who walks in wisdom." Proverbs 28:26

Our minds have more capability than the minds of animals but can degenerate into animal-like thinking. A story about King Nebuchadnezzar refers to him losing his mind and becoming animal-like in his thinking and actions. *"He was driven from among the children of humankind, and his mind was made like that of a beast, and his dwelling was with the wild donkeys." Daniel 5:21*

> The role of the mind (our ability to think) is to learn the truth and apply that truth to our desires—to sort out what will lead to good outcomes versus what will lead to disappointing results.

The role of the mind (our ability to think) is to learn the truth and apply that truth to our desires—to sort out what will lead to good outcomes versus what will lead to disappointing results. In God's evaluation preceding the flood, He concluded that the mind of His masterpiece creation, humanity, was not working correctly. We'll learn more about this in Chapter 4.

Next, we will explore what the mind produces—an intention.

Intention Precedes Action

In the Noah scene, as God evaluates humanity, He implies that what precedes actions are "intentions." The root word in Hebrew means something imagined or an idea. In several places in the Bible, this

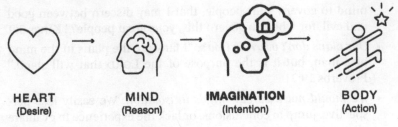

HEART	MIND	IMAGINATION	BODY
(Desire)	(Reason)	(Intention)	(Action)

FIGURE 2.3   The role of intention.

term is used to describe the work of a "potter," who shapes clay into a form. (See Figure 2.3.)

Similarly, we "form" an idea or intention in our mind, which leads to action. Our mind is where the jumble of thoughts and ideas takes shape into an imagined solution. It, too, brings order out of the chaos of ideas. This has been called the "first creation."

In continuing the thread of how we are like God, I am reminded of the following moving passage in Psalms 139 that declares God "intended" you. It refers to the creation of a child in the womb:

> *Your eyes saw my unformed substance; in your book were written, every one of them, the days that were formed for me, when as yet there were none of them.*
>   *How precious to me are your thoughts, O God! How vast is the sum of them!*

God thought of us before creating us. This passage celebrates God's intention, which led to our existence. We have this ability to imagine something before building it. And this imagination step is part of the creation process.

I have noticed that enthusiasm for action doesn't occur until someone has imagined a solution. There is little engagement by others when there is a lack of vision for what you are trying to do.

> **We have this ability to imagine something before building it. And this imagination step is part of the creation process.**

People imagine their own solutions or respond to the solutions imagined by others. Either way, people need the imagined idea to engage in action. As a leader, think about the power of a clearly stated intention, such as President Kennedy's "Land a man on the moon by the end of the decade" or Elon Musk's recent "One thousand ships to Mars."

As mentioned in Chapter 1, we had our own humble version of a transformative intention. We gave our small development team the charter to build a next-generation product on the Windows platform and complete it in two years with only six people as resources. That intention changed the course of our business.

Forming intention with careful thought is essential to overcome chaos versus being overcome by it. This is a critical understanding for leaders as they think about engaging people.

Action Precedes Results

Notice that in this model of human architecture, only actions are visible to others. What happens in our hearts, minds, and intentions is not visible to others. They become visible as we act in pursuit of our plan. Our actions can include sharing our intention with others to engage them. Or we may implement the plan ourselves before engaging others. (See Figure 2.4.)

> What happens in our hearts, minds, and intentions is not visible to others. They become visible as we act in pursuit of our plan.

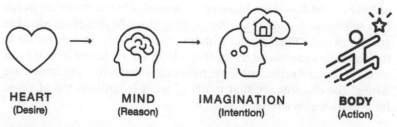

HEART (Desire)   **MIND** (Reason)   **IMAGINATION** (Intention)   **BODY** (Action)

FIGURE 2.4   The role of action.

The Bible refers to "bearing fruit" as an analogy to action. Continuing with the agricultural metaphor, the quality and type of fruit produced results from the quality of the seed, the soil, rains, etc.

Jesus taught about our actions (fruit). For example, he said (in Matthew 7): "A healthy tree cannot bear bad fruit, nor can a diseased tree bear good fruit." Notice that the tree represents the "whole" system, and fruit is part of that system. *The primary way to understand the system's health is by looking at the fruit it produces.* He is pointing out that rotten fruit is not the problem. Rotten fruit is *a symptom* of the system.

> The primary way to understand the system's health is by looking at the fruit it produces.

Said another way, our "fruit" results from the synergy among our desires, thoughts, imagination, and actions. Somehow, a single "seed" (a desire), mixed with imagination and hard work, can produce an abundance of fruit.

The action phase of our lives is fraught with challenges. Whereas desire, thought, and intention can happen in a few seconds, fulfilling that intention can take a lifetime.

Because our actions are visible to others, they are evaluated by default. They also allow us to see whether we got what we wanted. However, what is not as obvious is why we got what we did. Many hidden factors determine the effectiveness of our actions. Following are four example diagnostic questions to consider when we don't get what we want.

Were our "intentions" right?

If the design that led to the action is not good, you cannot make up for it with effort. This idea was reinforced by Peter Thiel (a founder of PayPal who has since invested in several other companies) in his best-selling book *Going from Zero to One*; there he describes what his associates call "Thiel's law," which states, "A start-up messed up at its foundation cannot be fixed" (page 105). I don't know if he is right about being unfixable, but his experience is that when intentions are wrong, the chances are that much of what is built on top of those intentions is also wrong.

Did we have the right skills?

Unless we have done something similar before, we don't know what it takes to get the job done. Eventually, you must bridge the gap between skill and intention. I think the saying in Texas is "All hat, no cattle" when you can't back up your intention with effective action.

Do we have enough resources?

You can't do most of the important things you intend to do alone. The creation narrative suggests that we cannot have dominion over the earth without working together. So achieving your goal requires the ability to get people to join your cause and orchestrate their efforts.

Do you want it enough to stick to it?

> When you form an intention, you are taking on the chaos of the unexpected. You commit to enduring things you didn't know, people acting in ways you didn't expect, and resources you need falling through.

I list this last—but for most dreams, it is the most important factor. When you form an intention, you are taking on the chaos of the unexpected. You commit to enduring things you didn't know, people acting in ways you didn't expect, and resources you need falling through.

The only thing that gets you through this chaos is undaunting will. Fortunately for humanity, God has given extraordinary levels of desire for different people and different purposes. I marvel at how my life has benefited from the desires acted on by those who have gone before me. I get to focus on what I do because others have built cars, roads, electrical grids, broadband, etc.

I hope this section on human architecture and the interaction of desire, thought, intention, and action has captured your attention. Leaders are responsible for bringing about action aligned with their mission ("good fruit").

How often do you wonder why people do what they do, and how you get them on the right track? This model helps explain unseen factors that shape a person's actions.

Next, in Chapter 3, we will explore three types of chaos that bring unique leadership challenges.

Takeaways

- The creator of something and the thing created have different purposes. The Bible tells us what the purpose of humans is.

- Since we are created in God's image, we can learn from how God did his creative work.

- Humans are created to exert dominion over the earth. This means to transform the chaotic resources around us and to serve our purposes.

- Humans cannot fulfill our dominion mission without working together.

- In enabling us to have dominion, God designed humans with an architecture that links the interaction among desire (heart), reason (mind), intent (imagination), and action.

- We have extraordinarily powerful desires to motivate us to have dominion. We have minds that can learn and apply reason to channel desire in the right direction.

- We can categorize desires into three types: power (the skill, resources to fulfill your desires), reproduction (family, belonging), and identity (understanding who you are, why you are here).

- Human reaction to not getting what we desire ranges from anger and fear to discouragement, envy, and other emotions.

CHAPTER 3

All Chaos Is Not Alike

The earth was without form and void, and darkness was over the face of the deep.

Genesis 1

My four grandsons, ages seven and under, spent the weekend at our house, and it was fun but chaotic. They argued for 20 minutes about which movie to watch, and then, five minutes into the movie, they were ready to do something else. After an hour, they had started 10 different games and finished none of them nor put them away—all normal but still chaotic.

We use the term *chaos* to reflect circumstances that are unpredictable and outside our control. There is even a field of mathematics that attempts to describe the unpredictable. Remember that the creation narrative in the Bible starts with chaos—"void and without form."

In this chapter, we will break down chaos into three classifications to make it easier to describe their differing aspects. We will also broaden the discussion to the benefits and the progressive nature of chaos.

Natural Chaos

From childhood, we discover things that happen in the world beyond our control. Insurance companies use the language "acts of God" to classify such events—weather, earthquakes, hurricanes. I refer to this category as natural chaos.

In 541 AD, the Justinian Plague killed 100 million people, estimated to be half the world's population—the deadliest plague in history. Transmitted by rodents, the plague spread rapidly. And it created economic, social, and political chaos for hundreds of years.

However, even though natural chaos is outside our control. That does not mean there is nothing we can do about it. In the Justinian Plague, eliminating the filthy conditions under which rats flourished was a choice society could make.

Another closer-to-home example is flooding. I live in a community in northwestern Ohio that sits on a river. Periodically, floods occur and do much damage. The community debates fiercely how to manage these surges. No one has suggested we can control the rains that cause them. But we have obvious choices about where to build homes or improve the capacity of waterways.

> Sometimes we fall into the trap of assuming that because we cannot control something, we can't manage it.

Sometimes we fall into the trap of assuming that because we cannot control something, we can't manage it. This fallacy emerges in the work world as I listen to people explain why they live with or accept the surrounding chaos.

For example, during department planning sessions, I have witnessed exchanges such as the following many times. The dialogue goes something like this:

LEADER: Susan, what are your goals for next quarter? Can you get the new training program built and rolled out by the end of the quarter?

SUSAN: Not sure. I get many requests for custom reports and other support issues, so I can't plan my work.

Left unchallenged, this kind of thinking justifies living with chaos instead of managing it. We turn into victims of the surrounding randomness instead of planning for it.

A different type of chaos is what I refer to as social chaos.

Social Chaos

Social chaos refers to the unpredictability rooted in interactions among people. I remember the professor in my first college sociology class stating that over the millennia, humankind had made immeasurable technological progress but no social progress.

> Over the millennia, humankind has made immeasurable technological progress but no social progress.

That was a new thought for me as a college freshman. As time has passed, I see the evidence for both statements. It raises the question, "Why?" As leaders, it is important to understand the answer to this question. We will explore this further as we progress through the book.

For most of us, when we refer to the chaos in our life, we are talking about the unpredictability of interactions with other people.

Some reasons for this are obvious. First, our population since 1900 has increased from 1.65 to 7.9 billion. (Figure 3.1 illustrates the rate of population increase since 1760.) As a result, there are more people, more interactions, and more confusion.

Second, every single person on earth has a unique combination of personality, background, and expectations. DNA researchers tell us that no two people are identical. Even identical twins have different DNA and fingerprints.

Third, with recent technological advances, we are confronted with our differences hundreds of times a day. A hundred years ago, people had far less contact with other individuals and cultures. Our differences weren't "in our faces" as much.

Because human interaction is such a broad topic, it is helpful to recognize there are many subcategories that we will not focus on in

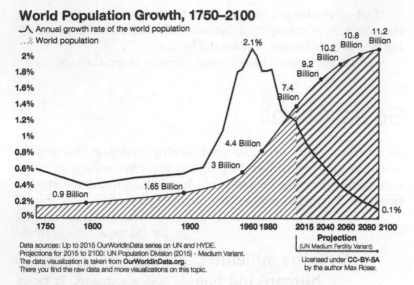

World Population Growth, 1750–2100

Data sources: Up to 2015 OurWorldInData series on UN and HYDE.
Projections for 2015 to 2100: UN Population Division (2015) - Medium Variant.
The data visualization is taken from **OurWorldInData.org**.
There you find the raw data and more visualizations on this topic.

FIGURE 3.1   World population growth—Our world in data.

this book. A few subcategories follow. They overlap, but our focus is on the chaos associated with human interaction at work, the third subcategory.

- Country specific—language, geographical, and cultural boundaries;
- Local communities—states, cities, neighborhoods;
- Work—organization-wide or workgroups within the organization;
- Families—immediate and extended.

Technological and economic changes over the past hundred years have sped up the rate of change in these subcategories. Ease of travel, immigration, the Internet, change in family structure, high-tech wars, and globalization of economic supply chains all affect the stability of human interaction.

The combination of geometric growth in population and geometric adoption of technology creates dynamics that have not occurred before in history.

If you are experiencing chaos at work, you are not alone. The CohnReznick research shows that 46% of people report that "chaos is pervasive" across their organization.

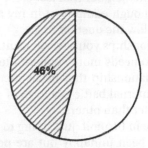

FIGURE 3.2 Pervasiveness of chaos.
Source: Eliminating Organizational Chaos (cohnreznick.com).

...geometric growth in population and geometric adoption of technology creates dynamics that have not occurred before in history.

Social chaos is inseparable from the next category (chaos within) since the interactions among people depend on what is happening inside the individuals in society.

Let's explore.

The Chaos Within

Most of us find it easier to talk about the confusion outside us than inside. It reminds me of a preacher I used to listen to who, when things got personal, would say with a smile, "Now you have gone from preaching to meddling."

I remember thinking I would have my act together when I was my father's age (mid-40s). I am well past that age and still waiting.

It is uncomfortable to probe the turmoil of desires, ideas, and half-formed thoughts inside us. As a teenager, I remember thinking I would have my act together when I was my father's age (mid-40s). I am well past that age and still waiting.

As described in Chapter 1, we all think we want things that our behavior contradicts. Remember that last piece of fitness equipment you bought? I have enough equipment in my attic to start a public gym. But I'd have to blow the dust off first.

What about relationships you say you want to improve? Perhaps you have a friend who needs more support after a difficult time. Or you have a family relationship that needs mending. What are you doing about it? This internal battle is a form of chaos. We all have it. Some of us hide it better than others.

Sometimes we are in turmoil, just trying to understand what we want. Have you ever been unhappy but are not sure why? Got up on the wrong side of the bed? I am glad to have a spouse who knows me well enough to cut me some slack in those periods. She doesn't allow my chaos to add to hers.

> Sometimes we are in turmoil, just trying to understand what we want. Have you ever been unhappy but are not sure why?

Usually, it is easier to focus on the inconsistencies in others. I notice this in my behavior as a parent. When he was thirteen, my oldest son was lobbying to spend some of his hard-earned money on the latest Xbox. We agreed on some goals that would allow him to buy one. The goals involved doing his schoolwork without being asked and achieving certain grades.

Within two days, he was shirking his homework. I asked him if he still wanted his Xbox. He said yes. I asked why he wasn't doing his homework. In a moment of openness, he said, "Dad, I just hate doing it." I appreciated his honesty. Welcome to life, son. I have the same problem.

Some of my double-mindedness reminds me of what neuroscientists call the "alien hand syndrome," where one hand acts independently of conscious thought. The BBC documentary *The Brain: A Secret History* reports one case where a patient, as part of severe epilepsy treatment, had the connection between the right and left hemispheres of their brain severed. After the surgery, one of their hands would try to slap the patient, and the other would stop it. We continue looking everywhere for explanations for our behavior, and this surgery example shows that we really are double-minded in some ways.

> We continue looking everywhere for explanations for our behavior, and this surgery example shows that we really are double-minded in some ways.

The Bible speaks directly to the benefit that occurs when our desires, reason, intentions, and actions align around good things—and, in contrast, what happens when they do not. In the next chapter, we'll dig into the biblical definitions of *good* and *evil* gaining surprising insight into the freedom *and* responsibility of a leader.

Our internal chaos has a direct relation to social chaos. Let's use an analogy of society as a living organization. Just as a stable body depends on having healthy cells, a stable society depends on having stable people.

It is easy to see the compounding effect of society being built on unpredictable individuals. It is amazing that eight billion people with unique desires function as well as we do. And if that weren't challenging enough, our desires continue to change.

You will lead yourself and others more effectively if you embrace the truth in this proverb: "The purpose in a person's heart is like deep water, but a person of understanding will draw it out" (Proverbs 20). We all need to become students of desire—both our desires and those of the people around us.

No one wants to do what they should do all the time. For many of us, making the cold calls required to grow sales isn't as easy (or fun) as charting growth in a spreadsheet and envisioning your commission. But, as Thomas Edison reminds us, "Vision without execution is a hallucination."

If you understand your tendency and the tendency of others not to do the things we know we should, you'll better understand what it means to lead yourself and others. This observation reminds me of a success story.

Self-Alignment Success Story

As a coach, I was dialoguing with a second-generation owner of a family business. He decided he wanted to take his business to another level of performance. So we conducted an analysis of what his stakeholders (employees and customers) thought of how well the business was performing.

He learned his employees were deeply upset with his lack of leadership and commitment to the organization. He was coming in late and leaving the office early to pursue his other interests. And his lack of engagement produced a growing disengagement throughout the company.

With this input as a motivator, he set out on a systematic program to improve his business, starting with improving himself. One immediate result was his own internal realignment, which spread to the rest of the organization.

It's great to have win over chaos, but bringing order out of one problem situation creates another level of chaos to manage.

Overcoming Chaos Brings New Chaos

In the Genesis narrative, God pronounces each stage of the new order as "good."

> *The earth brought forth vegetation, plants yielding seed*
> *according to their own kinds, and trees bearing fruit in which*
> *is their seed, each according to its kind. And God saw that*
> *it was good.*
>
> *Genesis 1*

So, from the designer's perspective, ordering this raw material into something new and useful is good.

And yet, based on our own observations of nature, we can deduce another important principle. As my dad used to tell me, "You fix one problem, you create another."

For example, during creation, adding all those living plants, trees, etc., brings order out of barren land, but now you have to take care of that "farm" if you want to eat from it. You've built something, and you have to maintain it. In God's case, He makes it our responsibility to manage the world He created.

Another more current example is home building. A lumber company harvests mature trees to make lumber. The sawmill cuts the lumber into certain sizes. This lumber inventory is much more organized than the forest it came from. But if I want to build a house, raw lumber is chaotic compared to reorganizing that lumber into walls, rooms, and a roof.

And so it continues. If I build a house, I now have an ordered "system" that will return to a chaotic state unless I invest in taking care of it. Every week for the past 30 years, I have traveled by an abandoned house. It is now in a state of almost total chaos, roof collapsed, walls rotted. It barely resembles the house it once was.

This principle clarifies that we can't eliminate chaos; we can only reorder it for some purpose. And in that new purpose, a higher order of chaos will occur for us to manage.

> ...we can't eliminate chaos; we can only reorder it for some purpose. And in that new purpose, a higher order of chaos will occur for us to manage.

The law of the conservation in physics states that "matter can neither be created nor destroyed." Could it be that this law of physics gives us some insight into our own role in the universe?

Yes, it does. We can't add or remove one atom from the universe, but we can repurpose the materials that are here. That's what we were created for.

Next, in Chapter 4, we will explore the most important tool we have for bringing order out of chaos.

Takeaways

- Chaos is not inherently bad; it is a resource that has not yet been applied to some purpose. For that reason, it is unordered and unpredictable.

- There are three categories of chaos—natural, social, and internal (the chaos within). Natural includes acts of nature outside our control. Social chaos is the unpredictable interactions among people, and the chaos within is internal misalignment among our desires and actions.

- Chaos always exists, we cannot eliminate it. When you bring order to one level of chaos (transform materials into a house) you just create another level to be managed (a house that has to be maintained).

- Embrace the chaos. You were created to overcome it.

CHAPTER 4

Purpose Is Your First Responsibility

May He grant you your heart's desire and fulfill all your plans!

Psalms 20

I n the previous chapter, we introduced the purpose of humanity, which is to rule over the chaos around us. And we introduced how we are built to fulfill that mandate through the interaction among heart, mind, intention, and action.

In this chapter, we will dig into the essential role of purpose in overcoming chaos. Effective leaders must understand the importance of determining a clear purpose to master chaos. Not only does the purpose have to be clear, but it has to be good, which is another leadership responsibility we will explore.

Let's start with terminology.

Don't Get Hung Up on Terminology

In Chapter 2, we introduced the diagram shown in Figure 4.1 to represent human architecture.

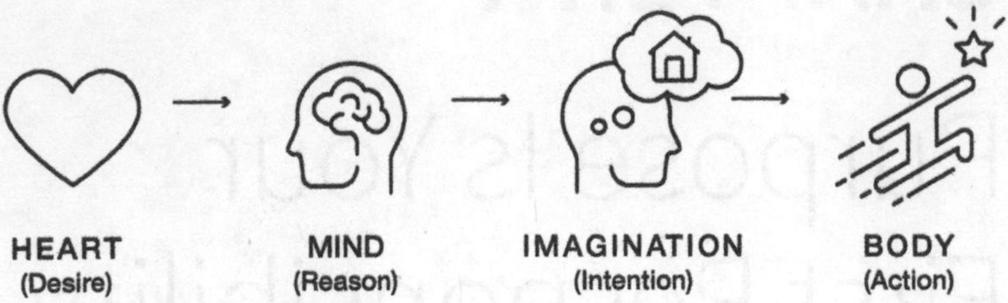

HEART
(Desire)

MIND
(Reason)

IMAGINATION
(Intention)

BODY
(Action)

FIGURE 4.1 Human architecture.

Unfortunately, most of us use the same terms in different ways. Following is a simple example:

- Desire: What do I want?
  - I want to become more fit.
- Mind: Options for getting what I want:
  - Join a fitness club?
  - Take up jogging?
  - Buy a mountain bike?
- Intention: Decision envisioned:
  - Buy a mountain bike, ride three times a week for an hour
- Action:
  - Go shopping;
  - Start riding.

When I leave the house to go shopping for the day, my "purpose" is to find a mountain bike. However, you could also say my deeper purpose is to get more fit. In a sense, my purpose and my desire are synonymous.

Suppose someone runs into me at the mall and asks why I am out today. I would say, "I'm looking for a mountain bike."

We all use these same terms in different ways, and you can only tell what people mean by the context of the discussion.

The same is true in this book. Sometimes I refer to purpose as that initial desire part, but as leaders, we often give people an assignment that, to them, becomes a purpose—but behind it are deeper purposes.

Mostly, I use desire and purpose synonymously as the starting motive for action. But sometimes, it seems more natural and understandable for a purpose to express intention.

Enough on terminology. Let's think about what God did when He created us. He set up an interesting experiment.

God's Grand Experiment

Pretend you are God and want to create a world and give that world to your "invention" called humanity. And you have decided that you are giving humanity only one purpose—to be stewards (have dominion) of the world you are giving them. You create their world with an abundance of resources and endless opportunities to pursue, a rich but chaotic set of choices.

> As God, how would you go about designing humans? Would you create them with great freedom to pursue their mission, or would you make them controlled so nothing could go wrong?

As God, how would you go about designing humans? Would you create them with great freedom to pursue their mission, or would you make them controlled so nothing could go wrong? It's your creation; you can do what you want.

The Three Laws of Robotics

Isaac Asimov approached this question in his short story "Runaround" (1942). He introduced the idea of intelligent robots bound by only three laws:

First Law: A robot may not injure a human being or, through inaction, allow a human being to come to harm.

Second Law: A robot must obey the orders given by human beings except where such orders would conflict with the First Law.

Third Law: A robot must protect its existence if such protection does not conflict with the First or Second Law.

In Asimov's approach, the creators of the robots "programmed" the robots so they couldn't violate these principles.

Also, notice that the three laws protect their creator and serve his purposes. And the laws prevented the *created* from overruling the *creator*. (Coincidentally, scientists are having these very debates now about the role of artificial intelligence in our society. With rapid advances in AI, are we on a path to creating something we can't control?)

No Rules—Almost

The Bible shows what God decided. And with my limited mind, His decision seems like a grand experiment with substantial risk. Let's restate what we have learned so far:

- God created us in His likeness. And by example, we know He applies purpose to chaos and transforms it.
- He created the earth and told us our prime mission is to have dominion over it. Second, he told us to grow in numbers to fill the earth, implying that the only way to have dominion is to increase in number and work together.
- He designed us to be designers and gave us powerful desires, and he gave us the ability to reason (think) about how to pursue those desires and imagine a solution (intention). And last, he gave us the strength, will, and ability to work and learn so that we can build what we imagine.

> The Bible shows what God decided. And with my limited mind, His decision seems like a grand experiment with substantial risk.

There are a few restrictions God built into His experiment.

First, He limits the life of individuals to about 80 years. It's truly humbling that with all our labor, we leave this world the way we came in—with nothing.

Second, we can't violate the physical laws of the universe. He gives us free choice for our decisions, but He does not let us control the consequences of our decisions. We are free to jump

> He gives us free choice for our decisions, but He does not let us control the consequences of our decisions.

off a building, but we are not free to stop gravity from doing its thing. We are free to lie, steal, love, and hate, but we are not free from the consequences.

We are even free to reject God's existence during our time on this earth. The next chapter is devoted to the reality that our desires don't obey the laws of the universe, but the consequences of our actions do. As leaders, this is really important to wrap our minds around, so we will spend considerable time on it.

It's good I am not God. I would not have thought of this system. But as I think about it, there are similarities in free enterprise economies. You are free to start any business you like. You get to decide your customers, products, and services and make all the decisions related to how that enterprise works.

But you don't get to decide the result. Will investors invest, will customers buy, employees work, weather cooperate, government stay out of the way, etc.? If you fail, you are free to quit, blame someone else, or take what you learn and start over.

As I reflect on this "system" God has created, I like it. I like the idea of having the raw materials of chaos available to me. I like the idea of freedom to choose my purpose, and I like the idea that there are rules I don't control—constants on which I can depend. And I can fight those constants or learn how to turn them to my advantage.

Thinking about this reminds me of watching my kids having great fun when they were first introduced to the card game Texas Hold'em. For a couple of years, it was a rage among their friends, and I would hear the raucous games and the reasoning behind the candy bets they were making.

> I also remember, in a quieter moment, thinking about what they had to look forward to in life. A game with far higher stakes, which would last a lifetime.

I also remember, in a quieter moment, thinking about what they had to look forward to in life. A game with far higher stakes, which would last a lifetime.

An adventure of the highest order, called life, where each person gets to decide what is true and how to act on that truth but doesn't get to choose the *consequences*.

So how has this grand experiment worked out? Let's start with the Creator's perspective.

The Creator's Critique—(continued)

In Chapter 2, we recounted God's checking out His humanity project to see how it was going. We took a diversion there to dig deeper into human architecture. Let's pick up with God's reaction to how the architecture was working.

> The LORD saw that the wickedness of man (humanity) was great in the earth and that every intention of the thoughts of his heart was only evil continually.
>
> And the LORD was sorry that he had made man on the earth, and it grieved him to his heart.
>
> So, the LORD said, "I will blot out man whom I have created from the face of the land, man and animals and creeping things and birds of the heavens, for I am sorry that I have made them."
>
> *Genesis 6*

We see in God's view that something about the interaction of desire, thoughts, intention, and action was producing a "wicked" and "evil" result. What do these words mean?

In English, *wicked* and *evil* are two different words. However, in the original Hebrew language, they are the same word. The Hebrew word for *evil* and *wicked* conveys the imagery of something "rotting."

Let's use an apple as an example. This book is printed in black and white, but you can imagine a shiny, perfect, fresh red apple. It's crispy, juicy, and delicious.

As time passes, that same fruit, if not eaten, will rot and become squishy, brown, and even stink. If you let it rot long enough, it ceases to exist as fruit and becomes unrecognizable. (See Figure 4.2.)

FIGURE 4.2 Fresh apple and rotten apple.
Source: Tim UR/Adobe Stock and Severas/Getty Images.

What does this have to do with being evil? In the Bible, evil is tied to purpose. In this simple example, we all know what an apple is supposed to be, and when it rots, it no longer fulfills its designed purpose as a desirable food. In biblical terminology, it is evil. *Evil* is always defined in the context of purpose.

This example is too simple to explain all aspects of evil, but it introduces one idea. To understand what a rotten apple is, you must agree on what a good apple is. For something obvious, like fruit, what the apple should be is a given.

> To understand what a rotten apple is, you must agree on what a good apple is.

Most people would not give it a second thought, and we don't have disagreements about it. But we have much more complex examples where agreeing on the definition of *good* becomes a source of chaos.

That raises another question. Who decides what *good* means?

> That raises another question. Who decides what *good* means?

Let's explore this simple question. The answer is not so easy, or at least not easy to accept.

Who Decides What Is Good?

The collected works of impressionist painter Claude Monet (1840–1926) are valued today at many millions of dollars. I show an example of one of his works in Figure 4.3, in black and white. It doesn't do it justice because Monet is known for his use of color.

One time before an art show, he destroyed fifteen paintings that he didn't think were good enough.

Were they good enough? Should he have destroyed them? We do not have Monet's explanation of what was wrong with the paintings. Many of us would question his decision and have tried to persuade him not to destroy his work. But he created the paintings, and only he understood what was in his mind when he did so.

The Monet example highlights a profound question that affects the structure of society and how it works together. The answer will unfold throughout this book.

When it comes to art, most of us accept that it is the creator's choice to decide what *good* means. Their mind, their desire, sets the standard. And it is only in that context that evil is understood since *evil* means not fulfilling a purpose.

FIGURE 4.3 Monet *Water Lilies.*
Source: Joyofmuseums/Wikimedia Commons/CC BY-SA 4.0

> When it comes to art, most of us accept that it is the creator's choice to decide what *good* means. Their mind, their desire, sets the standard.

Monet destroyed those paintings because they did not fulfill his purpose. In contrast, buyers of art have their own set of purposes for what they are purchasing. It is a different purpose than that of the creator of the art and is subject to a different standard known only to the buyer.

Let's move on to another example of good versus evil in the engineering world, hopefully not as subjective as art.

Is this Bridge Safe?

Occasionally, a bridge collapse will make the news. If you dig into the story, the bridge may have "rotted"—decayed, rusted. In other cases, the bridge had design errors and would not deliver what the original specification called for. And finally, sometimes, the bridge works as designed but is used for something outside its purpose.

Living in a farm country, I grew up with small bridges over creeks. And those bridges had signs on them stating their weight limit (see Figure 4.4). Over time, as farm equipment grew in weight, the design of bridges became more of an issue. If there were a dispute about the bridge's safety, you would go to the county engineers who had the engineering specifications.

This example is much less subjective than the Monet example. A bridge is subject to the laws of physics and engineering standards. Its design requirements and specifications are documented, and most people accept the authority of who decides what *good* means for a bridge.

This does not mean there could not be design errors or implementation errors, or even misuse of the bridge. Of course, we could have disagreements about all those issues, but the original purpose of the bridge is not a source of debate.

Again, according to the underlying meaning of the word *evil* in the Bible, a bridge that ceases to deliver on its purpose is evil. We use the word *unsafe* or *structurally unsound*, but it is the same idea.

FIGURE 4.4 Small bridge with weight limit sign.
Source: Akchamczuk/Getty Images.

Let's move on to an example with orders of magnitude more complex, the tragic example of the *Challenger* space shuttle. The US space shuttle had 2.5 million parts and is the most complicated machine ever made.

The *Challenger* Seven

In 1986, the space shuttle *Challenger* exploded shortly after the launch, killing all seven crew members (see Figure 4.5). The technical cause of the explosion was conclusive. The O-rings used in the shuttle did not seal the joints between the booster rocket segments, and the resulting leakage caused the explosion.

Were the O-rings good or bad? It turns out they

> Were the O-rings good or bad? It turns out they operated per specification. They were designed to work within a certain temperature range.

FIGURE 4.5 The *Challenger* disaster.
Source: Kennedy Space Center / Wikimedia Commons / Public domain

operated per specification. They were designed to work within a certain temperature range, and the launch temperatures were way outside that range.

This example shows how organizations and societies struggle with decision-making as complexity increases. We don't agree on the definition of *good*, and we don't agree on how to evaluate whether something is good.

In the shuttle's case, since there are 2.3 million parts, there is the question of what *good* means for every part. And there is the question of the shuttle's purpose, with all 2.3 parts integrated into one machine.

The launch decision process has been the focus of most of the post-event analysis. Several parties were involved, including NASA management, Morton Thiokol management, and the engineers within Morton Thiokol who designed the rocket and the O-rings.

The obituary of Bob Ebeling, one of those engineers, tells of his lifelong guilt and grief over the decision to launch. The engineers understood, before the launch, that the temperatures were outside the design requirements for the O-ring. Following is an excerpt from that article:

> *Ebeling was a booster rocket engineer at NASA contractor Morton Thiokol in 1986. He and a handful of his colleagues worried that the cold temperatures the night before the Challenger was set to launch would harm the rubber O-ring seals and allow burning rocket fuel to leak out of booster joints, NPR reported.*
>
> *Ebeling warned his boss the morning before the launch of the dangers that could face the* Challenger *if it was sent into space that day. He collected data that illustrated the risks and spent hours arguing to postpone sending it and its seven astronauts into space.*
>
> *Serna said she also worked for NASA at the time and would carpool to work with him. The morning of the launch, Ebeling picked her up and beat his hand on the dashboard, angry he had not convinced NASA to postpone the launch.*
>
> *"Man who predicted space shuttle* Challenger *disaster dies" (AP News, 2016)*

In the shuttle case, those who decided to launch were not the designers of the O-rings. And rightfully so. There were 2.5 million pieces in the shuttle. Not every designer could be involved in the launch decision.

However, in this case, the O-ring issue was raised before the launch by the O-ring designers, and their input was overridden by some political considerations that became more important than the safe travel purpose of the shuttle. The purpose of the shuttle got co-opted by other priorities. This is a huge warning sign in decision-making and something for leaders to watch for.

> **Purpose is the basis for determining what is good and what is not.**

The range of illustrations, from the obvious rot of an apple to the subjective judgment of Monet to bridges with clear expectations to the extraordinary complexity of the shuttle program, conveys how critical it is to know who determines purpose. Purpose is the basis for determining what is good and what is not.

> Decisions that aren't aligned with the strategy cause "decay" and are the equivalent of "rot," or what the Bible labels as "evil."

> As the complexity of our endeavors increases or the subjectivity of the purpose increases, human chaos increases.

> But what if the purpose itself is not good? How do you determine that?

Organizational performance depends on a few key strategic decisions and thousands of detailed actions aligning with that strategy. Decisions that aren't aligned with the strategy cause "decay" and are the equivalent of "rot," or what the Bible labels as "evil." In the business world, we call it misalignment, confusion, and waste. If there is enough of it, we call it "chaos."

As the complexity of our endeavors increases or the subjectivity of the purpose increases, human chaos increases. Effective leaders ensure that the purpose is clear.

However, there is another aspect of evil that is even more challenging. So far, we have discussed whether the results produced by a project or design met its standard. But what if the purpose itself is not good? How do you determine that?

Is the Purpose Good?

For art, if I don't like the artist's purpose (their approach to art), the response is simple; I don't buy it, and that's the end.

The same is true of products in a free market. Don't like it? Don't buy it. But what about the purpose of an organization? What if you are not in alignment with the purpose of the organization you work for? Do you work for someone else? Start your own company? Become an obstructionist in the place you work?

> **What if you are not in alignment with the purpose of the organization you work for? Do you work for someone else? Start your own company? Become an obstructionist in the place you work?**

> **History teaches us that when purposes are not aligned with God's principles, they don't last.**

> **A leader's first responsibility in overcoming chaos is to get their purpose right and make it clear.**

Sometimes those options have big trade-offs. You have a family to provide for and no great alternative. So you put your family first, but inside you have internal misalignment, doing something that you think is wrong or maybe just not satisfying.

What if you live in a country whose direction you don't believe in? What are your choices? Try to change it? Leave it?

History is full of examples of how we respond to changing people's minds. We try education, persuasion, maybe indoctrination, or coercion through social or economic force, and ultimately escalate to violence. History teaches us that when purposes are not aligned with God's principles, they don't last. He set up the universe that way. But there may be a long delay before we see the consequences, which can deceive us. We will discuss this form of deception in Chapter 6.

A leader's first responsibility in overcoming chaos is to get their purpose right and make it clear. Doing so creates the framework for getting people aligned and engaged around something that matters. If the purpose isn't right, it won't last.

Fortunately, we have some inspiring examples. I have picked two for your encouragement.

Gregory Boyle, Los Angeles Gangs and Hope

Gregory Boyle has invested most of his life in helping people out of the gang life in Los Angeles. He tells this story in his book *Barking to the Choir*. The background is that Rogelio has come out of gang life and is working hard to go straight and be a good father. And the excerpt picks up with a scene at a public swimming pool.

A homie named Rogelio and his six-year-old son, Arturo, are in the public pool on a boiling August day. There are countless "cannonballs" and Arturo's endless rounds of "Do it again" at whatever thing Arturo finds delightful and wants his dad to repeat.

> *Rogelio, after years of gang involvement, is trying his unsteady hand at fatherhood and earning clean money. It is a suit that is beginning to fit him. Rogelio asks for a respite from the "Do it again" and flops down on his towel at the edge of the pool.*
>
> *Little Arturo swims toward his father and folds his arms at the pool's lip, facing him. They don't speak. Rogelio is lying on his stomach and sees that his kid's face is but two feet away from his. Finally, Arturo says, "Apa, when I have a son, I want to be a dad just like you."*
>
> *When Rogelio tells me (author Gregory Boyle) the story over the phone, this last line silences him. I wait. "What are you feeling right now, Mijo?" I ask. Rogelio pauses. Then, voice cracking, he says, "Chills."*
>
> Boyle, Gregory. Barking to the Choir: The Power of Radical Kinship *(p. 18). Simon & Schuster. Kindle Edition.*

If he had focused on the chaos of the entire world, he would have accomplished nothing.

Notice that out of all the chaos in the world, Gregory's purpose led him to focus on (1) gang life and (2) Los Angeles. If he had focused on the chaos of the entire world, he would have accomplished nothing. Instead, focusing his purpose on an area he knew and was passionate about was where the victory over chaos began.

To recap the formula: right purpose plus right place plus lifelong commitment equals lives changed and chaos diminished. Gregory got it right!

One Thousand Races Pushing a Wheelchair

Next, we'll look at a very different story about the power of human desire put into action. In 1962, Rick Hoyt was born a person with quadriplegia because of cerebral palsy. He learned to communicate through a computer by using a technology that allowed him to tap letters with head motions.

> God has placed in us an unquenchable type of power source called desire. It is God-like and can accomplish unbelievable things.

At age fifteen, he wanted to take part in a benefit for a classmate who had become paralyzed and asked his father, Dick, to help. That was the beginning of the story of their call to racing. Over the years, his father pushed Rick in a wheelchair in over one thousand races (see Figure 4.6). They raced in the Boston Marathon every year until 2014.

I heard about this story years ago, but reading Dick's obituary reminded me of the power of purpose. God has placed in us an unquenchable type of power source called desire. It is God-like and can accomplish unbelievable things.

Like Gregory in the previous example, Dick did not solve all the chaos in the world. Instead, he found one purpose close to home and devoted his life to that purpose. He brought order to his family and his part of this chaotic world.

This is leadership!

Before finishing this chapter, I need to point out how essential it is for a leader to be a good follower as well.

FIGURE 4.6 Dick Hoyt with son Rick.
Source: Boston Globe/Getty Images

To Lead, You Must Follow

Why?

Because one person cannot build a space shuttle, a house, a car, provide electricity to our homes, or fulfill almost every other dependency we have. To conquer chaos, we must work together, joining under a shared purpose. There is no other way.

Unfortunately, being willing to follow is not always enough. As organizations grow their ability to define and convey purpose erodes. We will discuss this more in Chapter 6.

This lack of clarity has a compounding effect. It becomes more difficult to build the right teams if you don't have a clear purpose.

The result is an increasing number of people who are not fulfilled in their work and half-hearted in their contributions or can even become at cross-purposes.

> ### Your authority is rooted in knowing who you are, why you are here, and where you are going.

Great leaders focus on understanding their purpose and how they fit into the bigger purpose so they can set direction for those who report to them. Your authority is rooted in knowing who you are, why you are here, and where you are going. If you don't get your purposes right, setting the purposes of those who report to you doesn't matter.

One of Jesus's arguments to his disciples for following Him was His claim of being the Son of God. In this claim, He established His authority and the reason for being worthy of trust. As C.S. Lewis said, it was an extreme statement, and either He was a lunatic, a liar, or the Lord.

> ### Who you trust and whose purposes you submit to determines the course of your life and fulfillment of your purposes.

Whether you accept that idea, the principle applies. Who you trust and whose purposes you submit to determines the course of your life and fulfillment of your purposes.

In the next chapter, we will move on from setting a purpose to the biggest challenge of all: getting people to work together, especially since people don't obey the laws of physics.

Takeaways

- Rather than strict control over our behavior, God gave us desire and reason to govern our actions.
- With freedom comes responsibility. We control our decisions but not the consequences.
- A deep principle is that whoever creates something is the one who evaluates whether it is good or not. This applies to people and to God.
- God uses the word *evil* to describe something that is not meeting its purpose. We use words such as *bad, awful, worthless*, etc. Something "good" is the opposite.
- When a single person creates a single object, evaluation of good is clear. But when we create something complex with varying opinions of purpose, determining what is good is difficult. Think government.
- Using a business example, if you create a company, you decide what its purpose is. You have many factors to weigh customers, employees, and investors—but it is your responsibility.
- You can't really know what is bad unless you know what *good* means. This means that leadership involves understanding purposes given to them by their boss and it means establishing purposes for those who report to them.
- For humans to work together, good leadership requires being good followers as well. When you form a relationship at work, family or church, you are deciding to align some part of your own purposes with the purposes of that organization.
- Bottom line, you overcome chaos with purpose, and determining purpose is a leader's first responsibility.

CHAPTER 5

People Don't Obey the Laws of Physics

And if a house is divided against itself,
that house will not be able to stand.

Mark 3

The creation narrative hints at a paradox that was built into human design. The paradox is this. Humans were created to have dominion over the whole earth, *but* we have to work with other people to do it, and we don't know how. Very few civilizations have been able to hold together longer than 10 generations.

> The paradox is this. Humans were created to have dominion over the whole earth, *but* we have to work with other people to do it, and we don't know how.

In this chapter, we will move from the importance of purpose to the importance of "oneness"—the realization that a leader's most difficult challenge is *how* to put the pieces (people) together into an integrated whole and to keep them together.

This was the most challenging chapter for me to write, and it will probably be the most difficult to grasp the meaning behind my words.

The Bible reserves a special place for the concept of oneness. God declares Himself to be "one" (Father, Son, and Holy Spirit). He declares that man and woman become "one" in marriage, and finally, He says that the church is "one."

To get the proper perspective of the magnitude of the challenge facing leaders, I need to drill into how God integrated parts of the universe. I will finish the chapter by describing why leadership in yourself and others is critical to all humanity.

Let's start in a strange place: the make-up of atoms in the universe. We'll then proceed to the structure of human cells, the human body, the role of time, and wisdom and get to the point of the chapter at the end.

There's a Pony in Here Somewhere

Genesis states that God created the heavens and the earth in an "unformed" state before transforming them. What was that unformed state like? I don't know. But scientists know something about the matter in our universe today. Let's start there.

Scientists tell us that visible matter in the universe consists of atoms, which are made up of neutrons, protons, and electrons. There is evidence that there are even smaller particles. For my layperson's illustration, I will make my point with atoms.

The chart shown in Figure 5.1 documents the distribution of the elements in the universe. A whopping 98% of all atoms are two elements—hydrogen at 73.9% and helium at 24%. We know from our high school chemistry classes that over one hundred other elements exist. The remaining elements account for about 2% of the atom population.

> As I look at the variety of shapes, smells, tastes, and textures of living and inorganic things in our world, I would never guess that they could have originated from such a short list of raw materials.

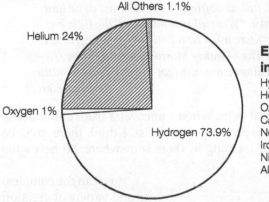

All Others 1.1%

Helium 24%

Oxygen 1%

Hydrogen 73.9%

Element Abundance in the Universe
Hydrogen: 73.9%
Helium: 24.0%
Oxygen: 1.0%
Carbon: 0.5%
Neon: 0.1%
Iron: 0.1%
Nitrogen: 0.1%
All Others: 0.3%

FIGURE 5.1   Atom population of the universe.

I am not a physicist or chemist, and this surprises me.

As I look at the variety of shapes, smells, tastes, and textures of living and inorganic things in our world, I would never guess that they could have originated from such a short list of raw materials.

My reaction to this surprise is illustrated by a very old joke about six-year-old twin boys. This joke was a favorite of President Ronald Reagan, who retold it often.

Worried that the boys had developed extreme personalities—one was a total pessimist, the other a total optimist—their parents took them to a psychiatrist.

First, the psychiatrist treated the pessimist. Trying to brighten his outlook, the psychiatrist took him to a room piled to the ceiling with brand-new toys. But instead of yelping with delight, the little boy burst into tears. "What's the matter?" the psychiatrist asked, baffled. "Don't you want to play with any of the toys?" "Yes," the little boy bawled, "but if I did, I'd only break them."

Next, the psychiatrist treated the optimist. Trying to dampen his outlook, the psychiatrist took him to a room piled to the ceiling with horse manure. But instead of wrinkling his nose in disgust, the optimist emitted just the yelp of delight the psychiatrist had been hoping to hear from his brother, the pessimist. Then he clambered to the top of the pile, dropped to his knees, and began gleefully digging out scoop after scoop with his bare hands. "What do you think you're doing?" the

psychiatrist asked, just as baffled by the optimist as he had been by the pessimist. "With all this manure," the little boy replied, beaming, "there must be a pony in here somewhere!"
The Monday Morning Memo (https://www .mondaymorningmemo.com/got-to-be-a-pony-in-hither- somewhere/)

I am like the second twin. When I uncover a truth dramatically different from what I expect, as an optimist, I think there must be a significant nugget of learning in there somewhere. So here's the obvious question.

> How can the complexity and variety of creation originate from only two types of atoms? Is there a hint of a principle that applies to leadership in this?

How can the complexity and variety of creation originate from only two types of atoms? Is there a hint of a principle that applies to leadership in this?

Let's dig deeper. There are more surprises in the way God created things. And I promise they have relevance to leadership.

Order Matters More than Inputs

Scientists also explain that Einstein's famous equation, $E = mc^2$, expresses the equivalence between mass and energy. E stands for energy, m for mass, and c for the speed of light. Since the speed of light is 299,792,458 meters per second, this equation tells us there is a huge amount of energy in a small amount of mass.

On the positive side, this explains why nuclear power plants can power a city with a small amount of matter. On the other end of the spectrum, this is also how we can level an entire city with two pounds of uranium.

The universe's construction provides a major hint that building things is not so much about the raw materials used. Instead, it is about *how those materials are assembled.*

Bear with me a little longer. We are digging deep into the physics of the universe because we are created in God's image. By understanding

> The universe's construction provides a major hint that building things is not so much about the raw materials used. Instead, it is about *how those materials are assembled.*

the Creation, we learn more about the nature of God. If we are created in His image, we should be able to learn from how He does His work.

We still have a little way to go in chemistry and biology. I am making the case with seldom understood reasons why leadership is such incredibly important work and why it is difficult to do well.

Let's get more specific about another integration masterpiece—a living human cell.

A Cell Is More Complex than New York City

According to estimates made by engineers at Washington University, there are about one hundred trillion cells in the human body and about one hundred trillion atoms within *each* cell. ("How Many Atoms Are There in a Human Cell?" https://www.thoughtco.com/how-many-atoms-in-human-cell-603882#:~:text=Scientists%20estimate%20the%20average%20cell, of%20cells%20in%20the%20body.)

Each cell is a fantastic piece of engineering. They are like tiny factories with the equivalent of gears, transportation systems, and communication systems, as illustrated in Figure 5.2. One hundred trillion atoms work together to function as a single cell. That's integration! Linus Pauling said, "Just one living cell in the human body is more complex than New York City."

> Linus Pauling said, "Just one living cell in the human body is more complex than New York City."

So what can I learn from the intricacy of the human cell? It takes one

Animal Cell

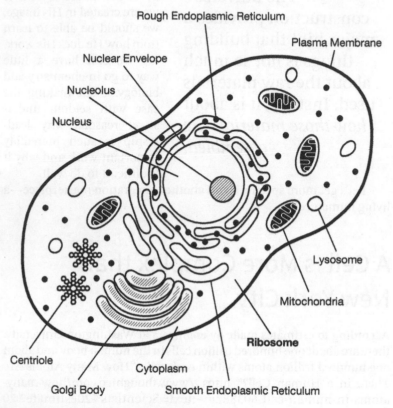

FIGURE 5.2 Animal cell structure.
Source: webstockreview.net.

hundred trillion atoms to build one, and it has lots of small, highly functional parts, so this integration has to be based on a very sophisticated design.

Let's take this management analogy one step further to consider how cells are integrated into the human body, which is analogous to an organization.

I am building the case that integrating people into an organization around a shared purpose is the most challenging work there is. And by studying God's supreme example of integration, the human body, we can learn something really important about leadership.

Three Buckets of Coal and a Bucket of Water

We know from the creation narrative that God first created a lot of rocks, water, and other inorganic matter from the chaos. Humanity has figured out how to do similar things on a much smaller scale.

For example, we can make concrete by combining sand, rock, and cement. But creating rocks that don't reproduce is one thing; creating something living is in a different category of integration altogether.

Nothing in creation compares to the human body. A cell from a father and a mother combines into a single cell, reproducing and differentiating into different organs and systems until a grown human has one hundred trillion cells, each of which has one hundred trillion atoms. The complexity factor is way beyond our ability to comprehend.

But wait, there is another surprise here. The human body is about 75% hydrogen and oxygen (water) and 23% carbon, with a few other trace elements added. Similar to the universe, which is composed of 98% of two elements, the human body is composed of 98% of three simple elements.

As a note to those of you who are paying attention, you may be thinking, "Wait a minute, I thought you said the universe is 98% hydrogen and helium. How can the human body be 98% carbon and water?" The answer is that God uses the heat of stars to generate other elements from hydrogen and helium in sufficient quantities to create planets and people.

Let's return to the human body. I offer the following anecdote (illustrated in Figure 5.3) to convey the importance of integration. For a 150-pound person, the only difference between three five-gallon buckets of water and a bucket of coal (shown on the left) and a person (on the right) is **the way** these 10,000,000,000, 000,000,000,000,000,000 atoms integrate.

> How is it possible that the same raw materials turn into something so radically different based on how they are arranged? Again, this highlights the role of integration and design in bringing order out of chaos.

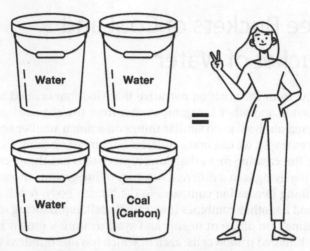

FIGURE 5.3 Three buckets of water and a bucket of coal.

There seems to be another "pony" here. How is it possible that the same raw materials turn into something so radically different based on how they are arranged? Again, this highlights the role of integration and design in bringing order out of chaos.

So far, we have talked a lot about integration, but we haven't emphasized design. Integration is putting things together in the right way. Design tells us what the "right" way is.

For the human body, scientists have made great progress in understanding where this design is stored.

Shakespeare in Every Cell

About sixty years ago, scientists Watson and Crick discovered that DNA in the human cell is the design repository. Every human cell contains a complete copy of the blueprint for how to assemble all the atoms in the human body. This would be the equivalent of having a copy of the complete works of Shakespeare in each cell (see Figure 5.4). (How Many Pages in A Gigabyte? A Litigator's Guide. https://www. digitalwarroom.com/blog/how-many-pages-in-a-gigabyte.)

This storage system is a technological marvel. According to researchers at Boise State University, DNA's "volumetric storage density is one thousand times greater, and its energy of operation is one hundred million times less than flash memory." ("'Data is

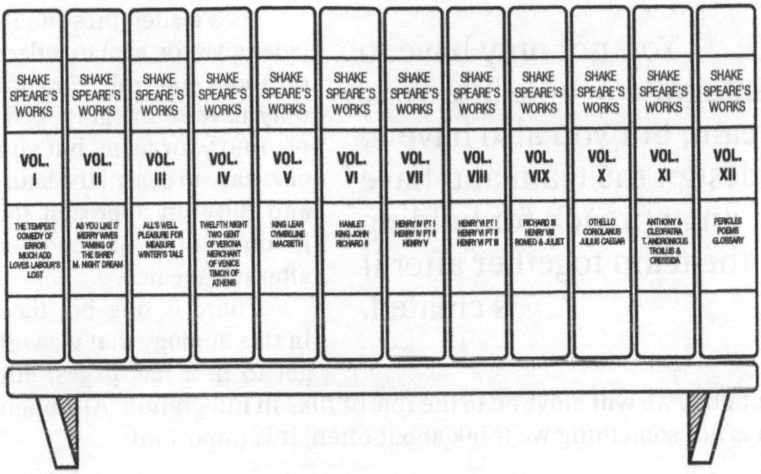

FIGURE 5.4 The works of Shakespeare.

in our DNA': Researchers advance DNA as a memory material." Boise State News, April 22, 2021. https://www.boisestate.edu/news/2021/04/22/data-is-in-our-dna-researchers-advance-dna-as-a-memory-material.)

On top of assembling our body in the first place, our bodies replace many of our cells over a seven-year cycle for as long as we live. So not only are trillions of cells assembled correctly once, they are replaced 10 to 12 times in an average lifetime.

For the body to make this happen, it requires food as raw material and a source of energy. It requires the DNA to build a cell and a way for cells to replicate.

It's important to mention that in these examples, the universe, atoms, cells, and the human body depend on the bonding forces that hold these things together. Remember that atoms are mostly empty space, so it is energy that holds them together.

It's important to mention that in these examples, the universe, atoms, cells, and the human body depend on the bonding forces that hold these things together.

> You not only have to integrate people into your team, but you also have to design the team and have an approach for holding the team together after it is created.

As a leader, these analogies give you a lot to reflect on about your role. You not only have to integrate people into your team, but you also have to design the team and have an approach for holding the team together after it is created.

There is one big flaw in this analogy that we will get to in a few pages, but for now, we will move on to the role of *time* in integration. Although it is not something we think about often, it is important.

It's about Time

The *Merriam-Webster Dictionary* definition of *time* is:

A nonspatial continuum that is measured in terms of events which succeed one another from past through present to future.

As you can tell from this definition, we don't know how to define time. The best we can do is illustrate it as something that separates the occurrence of two events. Even though we don't understand what time is, we know it is so fundamental to our definition of reality that Einstein references the universe as being describable only in "space-time" terms.

> We don't know how to define time. The best we can do is illustrate it as something that separates the occurrence of two events.

Time is a factor in everything we do. Time exists to allow things to occur in sequence. The creation narrative is ordered. One step occurred ahead of another. It would not have worked to create humanity first and then the world in which we live.

This principle is everywhere. We just don't think about it. We stand up before we walk. We bake the cake before we frost it. In human development, one cell leads to two, then two to four, etc. Timed sequence matters!

Integration depends on sequence, and sequence depends on time. As we prepare to think about how to build teams that function together, we highlight that getting the timing right is part of the process. This will become more clear in Part 2.

Since sequence matters, let's explore what God created first. In the Bible, the learning model builds one truth on another in the right sequence. So it makes sense to understand the very first thing that God created. It wasn't the chaos mentioned in the creation narrative. The first verse in the Bible doesn't tell the whole story. To get that answer, we have to look elsewhere.

> So it makes sense to understand the very first thing that God created. It wasn't the chaos mentioned in the creation narrative. The first verse in the Bible doesn't tell the whole story.

Wisdom Came First

About halfway through the Bible in the book of Proverbs, the following passage personifies "wisdom." It reveals that God created wisdom *before* He created the earth. Wisdom was present as a "master workman" during the process of creation.

> The LORD possessed me in the beginning of his way, before his works of old. I was set up from everlasting, from the beginning, before even the earth was. When there were no depths, I was brought forth; when there were no fountains abounding with water. Before the mountains were settled, before the hills was, I brought forth: While yet he had not made the earth, nor the fields, nor the highest part of the dust of the world.
>
> *Proverbs 8*

Wisdom is understanding how to apply truth to the right purpose and achieve something good.

Wisdom (being wise) is a central theme in the Bible, referenced over 450 times. Wisdom is understanding how to apply truth to the right purpose and achieve something good. Before creating the universe, God established a set of truths governing its creation. We are still discovering these rules, and they can't be violated.

In his book *Just Six Numbers: The Deep Forces that Shape the Universe,* Martin Rees says six numbers "constitute a recipe" for a universe. For those of you who are interested, I have listed them. I don't understand these actual numbers, but I do understand the deeper implication to leadership in Rees's premise.

The design of the universe is so sensitive to their values that if any of them were to be "untuned," there would be no stars and no life.

1. The number of spatial dimensions we live in: three.

2. The relative strength of the electrostatic to the gravitational force between two protons. This is a very large number, approximately 10^{36}.

3. The fraction of mass converted to energy when hydrogen is fused to form helium—approximately 0.007.

4. The average matter density of the universe, rather than being expressed in kilograms per cubic meter, is expressed in units where the critical density (10^{-26} kilograms per cubic meter) is equal to one—approximately 0.32.

5. The average dark energy density of the universe, also expressed in units where the critical density is equal to one—0.68.

6. The final number is a measure of how tightly bound the large clusters and superclusters of galaxies are. On the scale used in Rees's book, it has the value 10^{-5}.

Rees attributes this design to chance and not to a creator, but he acknowledges the universe is built around certain parameters that cannot be violated.

> The story of creation is not about matter; it is about the wisdom to integrate matter.

Before we continue, let's return to the Proverbs passage I cited earlier. It states that God created wisdom before creation itself. He established the framework and principles of how it would work.

Wisdom is the answer to the mystery of how a few basic elements can become something so complex as the human body.

The story of creation is not about matter; it is about the wisdom to integrate matter. There is a corollary to this for leaders, which leads us to the whole point of this chapter.

The Essence of Leadership

Leadership, the pursuit of purpose, is more about how we use the resources available to us than what resources we have available. Said another way, we are limited more by the wisdom required to get people to work together toward a shared purpose than we are by getting the exact right resource.

> ...we are limited more by the wisdom required to get people to work together toward a shared purpose than we are by getting the exact right resource.

To be clear, I am *not* saying that finding the right people is not important. Being a CEO for forty years makes it very clear how challenging it is to find people that fit.

I am saying that the greater leadership challenge over the long term is getting people to work together and keeping them aligned to a shared purpose. This is where the sustainability battle against chaos is won or lost.

What makes leadership so challenging and rewarding is that, unlike cells in the human body, the people who make up organizations

> What makes leadership so challenging and rewarding is that, unlike cells in the human body, the people who make up organizations are not governed by the laws of physics.

> consider how well your body would function if every cell in your body had a mind of its own. It would not be pretty.

are not governed by the laws of physics.

To let this sink in, consider how well your body would function if every cell in your body had a mind of its own. It would not be pretty. The noise of one hundred trillion cells arguing with each other would be deafening.

This is what is so profound about the creation story. It tells us God created us to have dominion over the whole earth, *but* we have to work together to do it. And history shows we cannot do this any better now than we were since the beginning.

There has never been a time when leadership is more important to society. When you undertake to lead well, whether at work or at home, you are doing heroically important and difficult work.

Closing the Loop

Before ending this chapter, I want to tie together two leadership responsibilities: getting purpose right (the previous chapter) and integrating resources to achieve that purpose (this chapter).

It's like the old debate about which is more important: the heart or the brain? It is a meaningless question. One cannot function without the other. Great execution with wrong purpose or great purpose with no execution? No one wants either.

The twentieth century boasted the greatest technological advances in history, yet we killed over one hundred million people in wars alone. This does not include murders, starvation, and other

> The twentieth century boasted the greatest technological advances in history, yet we killed over one hundred million people in wars alone.

avoidable deaths. Clearly, we still have a lot of room to grow to get both purpose and execution right.

But with effective leadership, we can bring some order to our part of the chaos and have an impact. Just like Gregory Boyle and Dick Hoyt did in the previous chapter, find your place and lead!

Next comes the last chapter in Part 1. Chapter 6 makes the case that even though bringing order out of chaos is challenging, another aspect of leadership is even more challenging.

Takeaways

- It is a paradox that we have the ability to rule over the whole earth, but we have to work together to do it.

- The construction of the universe hints that the essence of leadership is knowing how to order and arrange (integrate) the raw materials of chaos.

- The human body is a masterpiece of integration involving trillions of atoms, but at least each of those atoms obey the laws of physics.

- When building organizations we are integrating people each who has desires of their own that do *not* obey the laws of physics.

- Effective leadership involves getting purpose right, assembling the right people into a team, and doing the right things in the right order. And the more people that are involved, the more you can accomplish and the more difficult it becomes.

CHAPTER 6

Order Is Easier to Create Than Keep

Catch the foxes for us,
the little foxes that spoil the vineyards,
for our vineyards are in blossom.

Song of Solomon 2

Hopefully, by this point in the book, you, as a leader, have more appreciation for the importance and the challenge of the work you and the people around you do. But there is another aspect of leadership that is even more difficult and that is the subject of this chapter.

The premise is this: It is more difficult to sustain something you have created than to create it. Nations rise and fall, companies come and go, churches flourish and die. Without diligent and wise effort, houses rot, marriages fail, and farmland turns to brush.

> The premise is this: It is more difficult to sustain something you have created than to create it.

When asked what kind of government the constitutional convention had created, Benjamin Franklin stated, "a republic *if* you can keep it." The 81-year-old Franklin understood the same principle this chapter addresses.

After years of struggle with England in a deadly war, the revolution birthed a nation. Although the war was chaotic, forming the nation was also chaotic. In Franklin's last speech to the Constitutional Convention, he said:

> *...when you assemble several men to have the advantage of their joint wisdom, you inevitably assemble with those men, their prejudices, passions, errors of opinion, local interests, and selfish views.*
>
> Constitution Center (https://constitutioncenter.org/learn/ educational-resources/historical-documents/perspectives-on- the-constitution-a-republic-if-you-can-keep-it)

He stated that what came out of all these deliberations was not perfect but was as good as any alternative that could be developed.

Although aware of the cost of forming the nation, his sentiment expressed in "a republic if you can keep it" warned that the most difficult task lay ahead—keeping that which was just created.

Four thousand years earlier, when Israel was going through its formation as a nation, God warned the people about their inability to keep what He was giving them. As protection, He slowed down the process so they could grow their capability to meet the challenge. In referring to Israel's enemies, God said:

> *I will not drive them out from before you in one year, lest the land becomes desolate, and the wild beasts multiply against you. Little by little I drive them out from before you until you have increased and possess the land.*
>
> Exodus 23:29

In my second book, *Execution Revolution*, I introduced the diagram in Figure 6.1, depicting four quadrants that organizations cycle through. The vertical dimension shows the strength of strategy, and the horizontal shows the strength of execution (of strategy). By strategy, we mean making choices about the mission, the markets served, and the organization's unique value add. Those choices create the

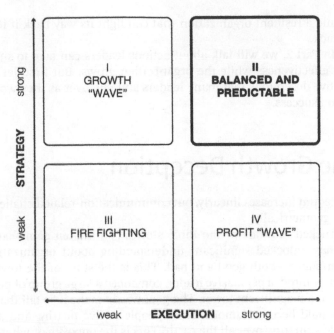

FIGURE 6.1   Strategy execution model.
Source: Gary Harpst (Author).

potential for growth. To realize the potential, the organization has to execute well.

Organizations cycle through these quadrants. As a start-up, growth occurs with a good idea and a small team. Execution is easier because everyone understands the strategy and is aligned around it.

As growth occurs, complexity increases and execution gets tougher. In response, leaders put systems and processes in place, and the organization may reach QII, balanced growth and execution for a while. Markets change, products age, and if the organization has not been changing, growth slows. In this period, the organization may maintain profitability for a season (QIV) because of reduced growth investment.

Underinvestment in growth leads to stagnation and re-entry into the firefighting quadrant. And the process starts all over.

Everyone would like to spend more time in QII. But no organization has ever stayed there indefinitely. However, there are ways to increase the percentage of time spent in QII. And there are ways to build a resilient organization that can fight its way back if it gets off track.

In Part 2, we will talk about actions leaders can take to sustain their effectiveness while the organization grows. But first, let's dig into five deceptions that many leaders stumble over as they work to sustain success.

The Growth Deception

Headcount increases linearly, but communication-related challenges grow geometrically.

Tucked into one of the Bible stories is a hidden gem that, for me, has unlocked significant understanding about organizational performance—both good and bad. This is the story of the tower of Babel. Nimrod, a persuasive leader, convinced a large group of people to build a magnificent tower. The goal was to make it so tall that the city would become famous, draw people to live nearby, and avoid people scattering over all the earth. This is the opposite of what God had instructed them to do: spread out and rule over the whole earth.

> **Behold, they are one people, and they have all one language, and this is only the beginning of what they will do. And nothing that they propose to do will now be impossible for them.**

God evaluates the situation and makes an interesting observation. He says, "Behold, they are one people, and they have all one language, and this is only the beginning of what they will do. And nothing that they propose to do will now be impossible for them."

God concludes that if they can continue to communicate and have a shared purpose, there is no limit to what they can do. Therefore, because their purposes were destructive, He hampers their communication by creating different languages.

Achieving our goals depends on effective communication. Since God is pointing out this principle, perhaps we should give it more attention. Most leaders acknowledge the importance of communication. Yet every organization we have worked with rates communication as its number one weakness. It raises the question of why this issue is so visible to leadership and yet so unresolved.

Execution Paradox

Exploring this question led me to the execution paradox, which I unpacked in my second book, *Execution Revolution*. This paradox states that every organization outgrows its ability to execute. Growth drives complexity, and complexity makes communication more difficult. The result is poor, chaotic performance and an organization that ceases to be "one" in purpose and execution.

> This paradox states that every organization outgrows its ability to execute.

The diagram below illustrates this challenge. Shown on the vertical axis is the number of potential interactions that exist in an organization. And the horizontal axis shows the number of people in the organization.

As Figure 6.2 shows, if you increase the number of people from three to 24, you have an eight-fold increase in headcount but a 117-fold increase in potential interactions. In this scenario, the complexity factor rises 15 times faster than the actual headcount.

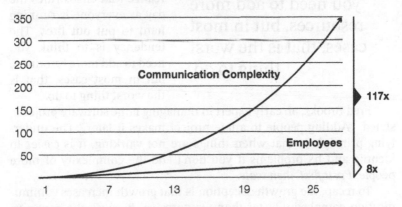

THE EXECUTION PARADOX

Communication Complexity

117x

Employees

8x

FIGURE 6.2   The execution paradox.
Source: Gary Harpst (Author).

> **Growth increases the illusion. More words, less understanding.**

Even though the language people are speaking has not changed, as the number of people in your organization increases, it sometimes feels as though you are speaking different languages. George Bernard Shaw had it right when he said, "The biggest problem with communication is the illusion that it has taken place."

Growth increases the illusion. More words, less understanding. Consider the following dynamics triggered by growth.

Headcount increase leads to more managers, which creates longer communication paths. Remember playing "telephone" in school, where the first person whispers a message to the next until what comes out at the other end is unrecognizable?

As new people join, they don't have the same understanding of how the organization works, its terminology, purposes, etc. Without historical context, words are not an adequate replacement for experience.

Specialization increases. Work completed by one person grows to need multiple departments to complete those same functions. Processes that worked well for one person don't work as well across departments.

> **The tendency is to think you need to add more resources, but in most cases, that is the worst thing to do.**

This erosion in alignment occurs gradually. One day, leaders wake up and realize that chaos rules the day as everyone is running hard to put out fires. The tendency is to think you need to add more resources, but in most cases, that is the worst thing to do.

Fred Brooks, an early expert in managing large software projects, stated, "Adding people to a late project makes it later." The underlying principle is that when things are not working, it is easier to identify and fix problems if you don't add the complexity of more people. *Fix it first, then scale.*

To recap, the growth deception is that growth increases communication complexity faster than we perceive. Because the corrosive effect is so subtle, leaders don't recognize the need to allocate the time and energy to offset this organizational entropy until it is out of control.

Let's move on to the next deception, which is related to time.

The Time Deception

The greater the period of time separating a decision from its consequences, the riskier the decision is, but for two different reasons—one obvious and one not so obvious. Let's explore.

A learning loop looks like the one in Figure 6.3. You have an idea, act on it, and learn from the results. We learn faster by doing *and* seeing the results. The obvious part of the risk is that with a long delay between decision and result, it will take a while to know whether the decision was right.

As time passes, we have other decisions dependent on the outcome of the first decision. So the first time-related risk has other

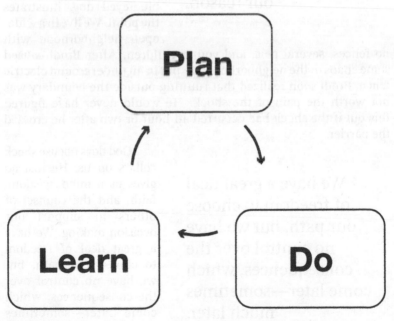

FIGURE 6.3   Learning loop.

cascading dependencies all based on an unknown future outcome. The greater the time until the result the more risk increases.

King Solomon highlights a second type of time risk in the Bible. He wrote about the time risk related to human desire in the book of Ecclesiastes chapter 8: "Because the sentence against an evil deed is not executed speedily, the heart of the children of man is fully set to do evil."

> ## We are creatures with powerful desires, and we depend on our minds to apply reason (wisdom) to our decisions. If the consequences are far away, our desires can easily overrule our reason.

Solomon speaks about the human tendency to give more weight to short-term benefits versus long-term costs. We are creatures with powerful desires, and we depend on our minds to apply reason (wisdom) to our decisions. If the consequences are far away, our desires can easily overrule our reason.

Brodi, my brown-and-blue-eyed dog, illustrates the point. We live in a wide-open neighborhood with no fences, several pets, and young children. After Brodi caused some chaos in the neighborhood, we put in an underground electric fence. Brodi soon realized that running outside the boundary was not worth the pain of the shock. He would never have figured this out if the shock had occurred an hour or two after he crossed the barrier.

> ## We have a great deal of freedom to choose our path, but we have no control over the consequences, which come later—sometimes much later.

God does not use shock collars on us. He instead gives us a mind, wisdom, faith, and the counsel of others to support our decision-making. We have a great deal of freedom to choose our path, but we have no control over the consequences, which come later—sometimes much later.

When leading yourself or others, this human freedom can manifest in different ways. Here are a few examples:

- Skip working out; health problems later;
- Borrow money to buy a new car—pleasure now, pay later;
- Sleep in today versus a bigger profit-sharing check a year from now;
- Hire someone who is not a good fit because of being short-handed; pay the price later when they can't do their job;
- Ramp up marketing to drive sales when the product isn't ready; revenue now, customer complaints and returns later.

The common trait of the examples above is that our desire to get something *now* is stronger than the consequences that come later. Somehow, time makes the reality of the eventual outcomes seem not as real.

As leaders, we are subject to this principle, and so are the people we manage. One way to cope with this is to create a business intelligence strategy where leading indicators guide short-term behavior to prepare for long-term results. Chapter 10 addresses this topic.

Tyranny of the Urgent

Another variant of the time deception happens in those situations where we know what to do, *but* many other urgent things are happening, and we think we still have time to do the right thing "tomorrow."

We fall into this trap because our brains go into automatic mode when pressed for time. We are usually right that we can push off an important item one day, but one day becomes five, then thirty, and we wake up and have a crisis on our hands.

A common example is putting off investment in relationships because they can wait "another day." As a father, I struggled with devoting time to our children in their early years. Finally, I committed to always be home by 6 p.m. with no exceptions, which helped avoid putting off the important during those critical early years.

As my children have grown into adults with lives of their own, I have had to change my strategy to schedule regular time with each of them. Otherwise, weeks turn into months, months into years, etc. Those of you who are project-driven know what a challenge this is.

> I include it not because you aren't familiar with it but because most of us don't apply it.

General Dwight D. Eisenhower created awareness of this principle of focusing on the important with his decision matrix. I include it not because you aren't familiar with it *but because most of us don't apply it.*

He would classify the items demanding his time into the following four categories (see Figure 6.4):

Important and urgent;

Important and not urgent;

Not important but urgent;

Not important and not urgent;

This tyranny of the urgent is just another form of time deception. The more significant issue is that we already know this is happening to us but seem helpless to address it. We'll learn more about that in Part 2 of the book, "What Effective Leaders Should Do."

The next deception affecting sustainability is related to how our brain works.

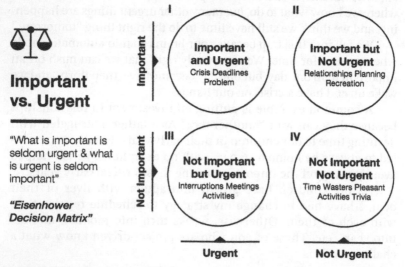

Important vs. Urgent

"What is important is seldom urgent & what is urgent is seldom important"

"Eisenhower Decision Matrix"

I

Important and Urgent
Crisis Deadlines Problem

II

Important but Not Urgent
Relationships Planning Recreation

III

Not Important but Urgent
Interruptions Meetings Activities

IV

Not Important Not Urgent
Time Wasters Pleasant Activities Trivia

Important — Not Important

Urgent — Not Urgent

FIGURE 6.4 Urgent versus important matrix.

The Perception Deception

The brain weighs about 2% of the body but consumes 20% of the energy.

Our brain—desires, reason, abilities, and learning—makes us unique as a species (see Figure 6.5). Leaders should understand the basics of how the brain affects our decision-making, whether good or bad.

The brain weighs about 2% of the body but consumes 20% of the energy. To conserve energy, it triages its seventy thousand thoughts a day into three processing areas optimized for distinct types of decisions. The three areas are:

Sub-conscious—e.g., breathing, walking;

Semi-conscious habits—e.g., driving a car, making a cup of coffee;

Intentional thinking—e.g., problem-solving, training, learning.

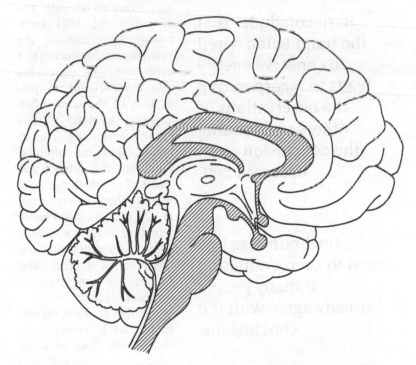

FIGURE 6.5 Human brain.

The implications of how the brain functions are explored in a fascinating book about decision-making by Dr. Gregory Berns. In *Iconoclast: A Neuroscientist Reveals How to Think Differently*, Berns reveals how the brain can believe a lie. He repeated the 1950s Asch Experiment (described below) but adds MRI imaging to improve understanding of what is happening during this experiment.

In the original experiment, several prearranged participants agree to give an incorrect answer to a question. However, one participant has received no advance instructions. The participants choose which of the lines A, B, or C on the card (shown in Figure 6.6) are the same length as the line on the left. The pre-arranged participants all answer incorrectly before the test subject answers. Burns reports: "Of the eighteen trials, the group is intentionally wrong on twelve."

When the prearranged group all agree on the *same* wrong answer, the control subject agrees 100% of the time. According to Berns, "Ever since Asch, most social psychologists have assumed that conformity is exerted at the decision-making stage in a sort of spineless capitulation to the majority."

In 2005 Berns repeated this experiment with the advantage of MRI technology. By examining the brain processing during this experiment, he concluded that the participant's perception of the truth often changed because of the group's influence. It was not a "spineless capitulation," but the subject was "seeing" something that wasn't there. Bern concludes that the brain being wired to conserve energy leads to incorporating the observations of others and treating the conclusion as an observed fact.

In the original experiment, Asch referred to this as the "law of large

> Bern concludes that the brain being wired to conserve energy leads to incorporating the observations of others and treating the conclusion as an observed fact.

> ...the brain sees less need to keep evaluating if many people already agree with the conclusions.

Asch Experiment

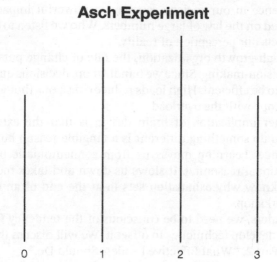

0   1   2   3

FIGURE 6.6 Asch experiment.
Source: Adapted from Gregory Burns (2010)/Harvard Business Publishing.

numbers," which says that the brain sees less need to keep evaluating if many people already agree with the conclusions. (Berns, Gregory. *Iconoclast: A Neuroscientist Reveals How to Think Differently* [Kindle Locations 1570–1575]. Harvard Business Review Press. Kindle edition.)

This means I can be "certain" of something that is not true. I experience this frequently as a leader. Often in a group meeting, we will discuss something as one item on a long agenda, we come to a consensus, and move on to the next item. However, when I am more relaxed at home or, as people say, in the shower, I realize I didn't really think about the decision. When I take time to think intentionally without the groupthink, I come to a different conclusion.

Although the law of large numbers is often helpful, these examples illustrate the opposite is also true. This brain shortcut can introduce deception. Social media, a relatively

> This means I can be "certain" of something that is not true. I experience this frequently as a leader.

new influence in our society, can have a powerful impact on our beliefs based on the law of large numbers. Who we listen to (and how often) affects our perception of reality.

In a high-growth organization, the rate of change puts pressure on our decision-making. Since we handle more decisions quickly, our brains try to be efficient. High loads reduce conscious thought to help the brain cope with the overload.

Another implication of brain design is that the extra energy required to do something different is a tangible reason busy people resist change. Learning moves us from semiautomatic processing into intentional reasoning. It slows us down and takes more effort. Now you know why exhaustion sets in at the end of an engaging, all-day workshop.

As leaders, we need to be conscious of the tendency for group-think and develop techniques to offset it. We will discuss those techniques in Part 2, "What Effective Leaders Should Do."

Let's shift to a different deception related to subtle changes in skill requirements.

The Skill Deception

As organizations grow, the requirements for a job can outgrow the skills of the person in the job.

Like any deception, these changes occur in nonobvious ways. Organization complexity grows much faster than headcount. We can see the headcount; we don't always see the complexity that comes with it.

Let's illustrate this with the diagram in Figure 6.7. On average, effective leaders can manage about seven to ten people. (This varies depending on the type of work, but for this discussion, let's use ten.)

At about ten people, a start-up organization adds its first leader of a department. A second layer begins. An organization of one hundred people will have about ten to twelve group leaders. At one thousand people, there are going to be about one hundred group leaders, which means three to four layers in the organization.

Because the organization is changing, the skills required to manage it also change. Five roles have to be filled in all organizations. In a start-up, these roles are not formally defined and are fulfilled by a few people handling multiple roles. The five roles are different

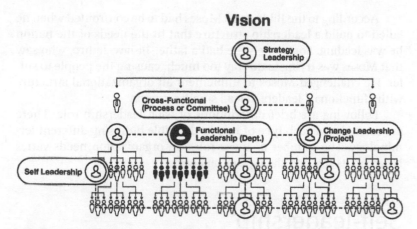

FIGURE 6.7   Organization structure.
Source: LeadFirst.ai.

> Because the organization is changing, the skills required to manage it also change.

categories of leadership—self, functional, process, change, and strategy. Roles are not the same as a job title. Most people serve in multiple roles. For example, everyone serves in a self-leadership role.

As the organization journeys from ten to one thousand employees, the one person handling sales and marketing in the ten-person company may now head up a whole division with separate sales, marketing, and communications departments.

If the original person responsible for sales and marketing is going to stay responsible for this function, they will have to develop functional leadership skills (managing departments), process skills (managing complex cross-functional departments), and change management skills (managing projects). Those capabilities weren't necessary when a handful of people coordinated everything, as in the beginning.

The skill deception occurs because the changes in leadership requirements come incrementally and, therefore, are less noticeable. As a result, communication and coordination breakdown, firefighting increases, and you wonder why things aren't working anymore.

According to the Bible, even Moses had to be confronted when he failed to build a leadership structure that fit the needs of the nation he was leading. Fortunately, he had a father-in-law, Jethro, who saw that Moses was trying to do way too much, causing the people to suffer. He challenged Moses to implement an organizational structure with "functional" leaders to lead smaller groups.

Following are brief descriptions of each leadership role. There are examples of each type of role in the Bible but using different terminology. The number of these roles an organization needs varies based on its size and the type of business.

Self-leadership

Self-leadership means living the character traits you would expect of a mature adult. Just as the human body's lowest unit of health is a cell, an organization's lowest unit of health is the individual. All other roles assume that the self-leader's traits are required for everyone. You can't lead others unless you can lead yourself. Example traits follow:

- Openness and honesty: the regular practice of speaking the truth and listening to truth in constructive ways;
- Integrity and trustworthiness: the character and competence to make and keep commitments;
- Emotional intelligence: the awareness of one's own emotions and those of others applied to building effective relationships;
- Action orientation: the ability to see what needs to be done and take action.

Functional Leadership

This skill emerges as departments organize around functional competencies such as sales, marketing, finance, production, and engineering. The person in this role understands the function, but they may have no experience managing others. Skills needed are:

- Planning: the ability to define how the group will achieve its mission with clear alignment and engagement of every individual and an approach for monitoring progress;

- Results oriented: the ability to coordinate day-to-day activities that produce planned results, identify necessary changes in plans, and communicate them;
- Teamwork: develop the synergy that only comes from a team working together on a shared purpose;
- Accountability: inspires excellence and roots out mediocrity;
- Ability to build leaders: invests and mentors people to prepare for the future.

Change Leadership

In a start-up, this is not a specialized function. Everything a start-up does is "change." But once an organization becomes departmentalized, change becomes more difficult. The reason is that most change needs to be cross-functional to be effective (see Figure 6.8).

And yet all the management communication and accountability infrastructure has grown around the functional departments. Functional leaders hire, pay, review, and manage all people from a functional perspective.

Project management is a mature discipline focused on effecting change. However, most organizations view it as a role that can be assumed by business functional managers. This may work for

Change Management Phase

Moving work groups through awareness, commitment, training and sustained practice (ACTAS)

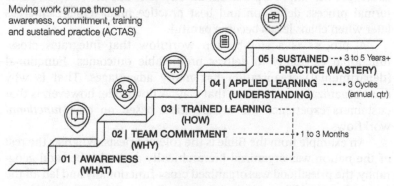

05 | SUSTAINED --▸ 3 to 5 Years+
PRACTICE (MASTERY)

04 | APPLIED LEARNING ----▸ 3 Cycles
(UNDERSTANDING)   (annual, qtr)

03 | TRAINED LEARNING ----
(HOW)

02 | TEAM COMMITMENT -----------┤▸ 1 to 3 Months
(WHY)

01 | AWARENESS ------------------------
(WHAT)

FIGURE 6.8   Change management model.
Source: LeadFirst.ai.

minor projects when the individual has the time to devote to project management. But for large, strategic, cross-functional projects, this approach leads to poor project execution.

The more complex organizations become, the more specialized are the project management skills required to drive change. A crude analogy is whether it would make sense to ask a general practitioner who sees a couple of dozen patients a day to perform an eight-hour brain surgery. There are two obvious problems: time available and skills required.

Following are basic project management skills:

- Project chartering: the first and most important skill—nailing down what success means for the project in measurable terms. If this is not knowable at the beginning, structure the project to figure it out or use an agile project management model.
- Project management: building plans, organizing resources, managing execution, reporting progress using resources who do not work for you.
- Implementation change management: crafting a strategy for introducing change into the organization at an appropriate time and pace while the organization continues to operate.

Process Leadership

Process leadership is the last formal skill to emerge. Every organization creates implied processes on day one, but the recognition of formal process definition and best practice management emerges later when chaos levels become painful.

A process is a step-by-step workflow that integrates cross-functional capability to deliver predictable outcomes. Functional (departmental) organization has many advantages. That is why most organizations structure that way. A downside, however, is that customers experience the organization based on *cross-functional* workflows.

An example from the Bible is the role of priests. Whereas the rest of the nation was organized hierarchically around tribes and geography, the priesthood was organized cross-functionally and led all the other "functions" in worship "processes."

As organizations grow, the functional structures become stronger and more entrenched, and the coherence of meeting customer needs decays. Organizations eventually wake up to realize that they need to manage processes like they do functional departments by assigning clear responsibilities and metrics.

Processes have most of the same organizational dynamics as cross-functional projects. Effective process management has people assigned from multiple functions that are not hired by nor report directly to the process leader. Processes differ from projects in that they are ongoing structures that last as long as needed. Projects should end. Processes focus on sustainability and predictability and are long-lasting. Projects focus on achieving one-time outcomes through one-time change. Cross-functional projects often create or reengineer processes that need to be managed from there forward.

Following are basic process management skills:

- Team formation: getting the right people who understand all the steps that are in or should be in the process;

- Change management: generating, evaluating, and implementing improvements and verifying results through measurement;

- Sustainability: monitoring and sustaining process performance;

- Team management: aligning, coordinating, and engaging people who don't work for you.

Strategy Leadership

Strategy leadership is the ability to define the vision and character of the organization. In successful start-ups, the founder brings this to the table. As the organization grows and the number of layers increases, the executive team becomes more involved in this process.

As alluded to earlier, Moses was in this function. He had the advantage of being chosen by God for his role and was given a vision and strategy. As his responsibilities grew, he had to change.

In the same way, the founder must adapt to the organization's changing needs or put someone with those skills in place. As a founder myself, I found this a challenging transition. What I used to do as a leader of a start-up, the things that got me where I was, no longer worked to go to the next level. And since I, and the surrounding people, had not done this before, it resulted in a lot of trial and error. The strategy leader role requires:

- Defining strategy: the purpose of the organization and clear vision that enable alignment by the rest of the organization;
- Developing executive leadership team: finding the right people and structure to guide the long-term development of the people and functions below them;
- Championing the mission: pointing people inside and outside the organization to the purpose of the organization and why it's different.

One clarification. Department heads or other leaders below the CEO still have a strategy leadership role in their departments. First they need to be able to understand and articulate organization strategy. *And* they need to craft a longer-term vision for their own department.

In conclusion, as organizations change imperceptibly, skill requirements are changing with them, also imperceptibly. Part 2 shows how to mitigate this reality.

Finally, we move into the last deception—desire.

The Desire Deception

Although much has already been said in the book about the role of desire in human behavior, this section focuses on the impact of desire that we don't detect. In this sense, it deceives us.

What we say we want is often not what we want. This reminds me of the debate we had as a group of teenagers around the campfire, solving the world's problems. The hypothesis put forward by Susan was that "people always do what they want."

> The hypothesis put forward by Susan was that "people always do what they want." This set off a firestorm of argument.

This set off a firestorm of argument. Martin countered with the example: "If someone puts a gun to my head and demands my wallet, I do not *want* to give it to them, but I will." Susan's comeback was. "You 'wanted' to live more than you wanted your wallet. You did what you wanted."

And so, the debate went on. I don't think anyone's mind changed that night, but the question of the role of desire in our lives is one that, for me, never goes away. The creation narrative suggests that desire and reason make us human—and the way we process desire and reason rarely works perfectly.

Unlike Susan, who said we always do what we want, the Bible acknowledges that we have two voices in our heads. For Bible readers, there is a well-known self-declaration of this issue by the apostle Paul. "For I delight in the law of God, in my inner being, but I see in my members (body) another law waging war against the law of my mind and making me captive to the law of sin that dwells in my members" (Romans 7).

On the one hand, Paul says he wants to align himself to God's purposes (law) in his inner being but recognizes he has another set of desires that are in conflict. He says that he wants to be "free" of this double-mindedness.

My premise is that you (and I) don't always do what you say you want to do. And sometimes you even deceive yourself by what you say you want. Your words declare what you think you want, but your actions prove you don't. This is the point Susan was making. If you don't recognize this in yourself, you won't diagnose that the problem is your desire, not your actions. This is the deception. When we don't like our actions or the actions of someone else, we often focus too much on the action and not nearly enough on the desire behind the action.

> And sometimes you even deceive yourself by what you say you want. Your words declare what you think you want, but your actions prove you don't.

Another twist on desire-related deception is how desires change. Somehow, when there is a crisis, the stress dynamic helps people align their desires with their actions. It could be a major competitive threat or excitement around a major new product rollout. These unifying times of focus can be fear-based, or they can be inspirational. The common element is that they help us get aligned internally and with other people. You can see why politicians say, "Never waste a good crisis."

However, as the crisis passes, the aligning force dissipates, internal misalignments surface, and organizational entropy grows into chaos. The deception is failing to understand that the alignment is temporary.

> This is *the* number one problem I see in the organizations I have worked with. People overestimate their will (desire) to make the changes required to keep chaos at bay.

This is *the* number one problem I see in the organizations I have worked with. People overestimate their will (desire) to make the changes required to keep chaos at bay. John Kotter, who has spent his life helping organizations change, says it this way:

> *Changing people's behavior: It's the most important challenge for businesses trying to compete in a turbulent world. The central issue is never strategy, structure, culture, or systems. The core of the matter is always about changing the behavior of people.*
>
> John P. Kotter, Dan Cohen. (2013). The Heart of Change: Real-Life Stories of How People Change Their Organizations, *p.11, Harvard Business Press*

The question we need to ask ourselves in a quiet place where no one else is influencing our thinking is, "Do I really want to change?" If you are like me, an honest answer can be sobering and maybe even discouraging. But start with honesty. Sometimes it helps to say aloud, "I just don't want to do what it takes to be a better

> The question we need to ask ourselves in a quiet place where no one else is influencing our thinking is, "Do I really want to change?"

> There is one industry that deals with this exact problem—helping people who are not doing what they say they want to do.

leader (or parent or you fill in the blank)."

No long-term change occurs without desire. The journey starts with being honest with yourself. Then decide where you want to go from there.

There is one industry that deals with this exact problem—helping people who are not doing what they say they want to do. Perhaps we can learn something from them that would work in our leadership roles.

Weight Watchers Speaks

I am fascinated by the Weight Watchers organization because of its model for helping people do what they already know how to do but don't do—take care of themselves. Weight Watchers' model is based on four key elements:

1. Method: an approach to eating, drinking water, and exercising that they teach. Thousands of programs would work but only if you pick one and stick to it.

2. Tracking system: a way for individuals to track whether they are following the "system."

3. Accountability: you can attend their meetings and get weighed or do it online, but you have a weekly check-in to see how you are doing. This is a biblical principle: "As iron sharpens iron so one person sharpens another" (Proverbs).

4. Community learning: you become part of a group that has made the same commitment you have. You share what works and what doesn't and encourage one another. Again, this is a biblical principle. If you are going to have "dominion," you must work with others to get it done.

I have personal experience with Weight Watchers that illustrates the challenge we face. In my early years in the program, I was traveling and often missed the check-in meetings.

After a while, I thought all they did was weigh me, record the result, tell me whether I was up or down, and charge me $15. It seemed logical to put a chart on my mirror, buy a scale for $25, and do it myself. It would save me a twenty-minute trip and $15.

You know the punch line already because, chances are, you are just like me. It didn't work. The program only worked for me *if* I submitted to their accountability. My self-discipline was not effective. You may not have this problem, but most people I know do.

As crazy as this behavior seems, the only thing crazier is not to admit that you behave this way. If you admit it, you can implement a mitigation strategy to offset your weakness. The alternative is to lie to yourself and never change. So the first step to success is to admit the way you are.

> As crazy as this behavior seems, the only thing crazier is not to admit that you behave this way.

The last two sentences above are a pretty good recap for this chapter. Several challenges make sustaining good leadership habits less likely. We are aware of most of them. The question is whether we will do anything about them.

We now move into Part 2, which provides specific recommendations for actions to take to grow into a stronger leader.

Takeaways

- As challenging as it is to order chaos into a functioning, purposeful endeavor, it is even more difficult to sustain it.
- Growth in headcount increases in linear fashion, but communication complexity grows geometrically. This erodes the ability to stay aligned in imperceptible ways that deceive leaders.
- As organizations grow, the time between a decision and its results lengthens. This slows down the learning and other decisions compound while waiting for the results.

- A related time deception is the human tendency to give more weight to near-term satisfaction than long-term results. Growth increases the likelihood that people are disconnected from the long-term results.
- Being overloaded increases the risk of groupthink. The brain conserves energy and when rushed, gives too much weight to group opinion instead of rational thought.
- Organization growth creates a complexity that requires new skills to lead effectively. Managers have to shift from being functional experts to management and team development experts.
- Leadership expertise requirements grow in five areas: self, functional, project, process, and strategic. The deception comes in that the skill requirements are rising with complexity, but it is not obvious to leaders that the gap is widening.

PART 2

What Effective Leaders Should Do

In Part 1 we established we are designed to overcome chaos and we do so by choosing purpose and aligning people and resources around that purpose. We also noted that it is more difficult to keep order than it is to build it. The high calling of leadership is to overcome those barriers and do it sustainably.

Parts 2 and 3 are organized around two dimensions of leadership development shown in the following image.

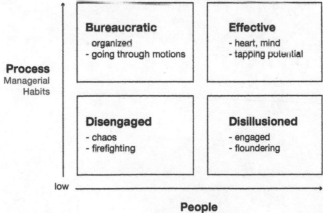

Sustainable Leadership Effectiveness

Bureaucratic
organized
- going through motions

Effective
- heart, mind
- tapping potential

Process
Managerial
Habits

Disengaged
- chaos
- firefighting

Disillusioned
- engaged
- floundering

low

People
Engagement Habits

The vertical dimension shows the managerial process habits that organizations need to establish. This is what Part 2 will address. People engagement habits, the horizontal dimension, will be covered in Part 3.

This diagram highlights that you need both capabilities to be effective. Process skills without people engagement is bureaucratic. And people skills become disillusioning if the processes don't provide some order. The two systems work together synergistically.

Part 2 is a compilation of managerial best practices that really need to become habits—the default way things are done in your organization. They include strategic planning, change management, operations management, continuous improvement, and talent management.

Part 2 chapters describe what leaders need to do:

7. Build a Habit-Reinforcing System

8. Set Vision

9. Prioritize Change

10. Balance Running and Changing

11. Get Results through Teamwork

12. Get Everyone Innovating

13. Prepare Their Team for the Future

After reading Part 2, you will have a much better understanding of what your own leadership system needs to do to support and build your leaders.

CHAPTER 7

Build a Habit-reinforcing System

*For the moment all discipline seems painful
rather than pleasant, but later it yields the peaceful
fruit of righteousness to those who have been trained
by it.*

Hebrews 12

In this chapter we will move from what leaders need to *know* to what leaders need to *do* to be effective.

And the first thing any organization that plans to grow needs to do is build a system that defines the way it will be managed. It has to create a framework that facilities leadership best practices and turns them into habits. I refer to this framework or platform as a "leadership system."

We will start by understanding why a habit-reinforcing system is needed and then describe five requirements that need to be satisfied when you build it.

Why Do I Need a System?

Organizations need a standard way to define priorities and manage execution with habits that use less energy so that discretionary mental bandwidth focuses on the more important work of leading people.

As you think about the nature of chaos, the design of people, the role of purpose, and the various deceptions covered in Part 1, you probably are coming up with your own reasons for developing some sort of approach to overcome these challenges. To aid you in your thinking, I give you four reasons to devote the time to develop your own leadership system.

1. *Free up time to focus on more important issues.* The brain only has so much bandwidth. An organization that does not have a standard way to manage the business is like having different keyboard designs on every computer. You spend all your time trying to find the right keys instead of the work you are actually doing. Today all of us type out of well-formed habit. We no longer think about it. Organizations need a standard way to define priorities and manage execution with habits that use less energy so that discretionary mental bandwidth focuses on the more important work of leading people.

2. *Engage people around purpose.* The purpose of your leadership system is to help people understand where the organization is going and how they fit in. Without some air traffic control equivalent it is difficult for people to understand how work is managed and how to do their own work well.

3. *Scale the business.* As the business grows, new people have to be integrated smoothly into the organization. Having a clear management model that people can be taught from day one speeds the process of integration and minimizes the dilution in purpose and strategy that growth can bring.

4. *Manage the leadership process just like any other strategic process.* To be managed well it needs to be defined and its effectiveness measured and continuously improved. This allows the process to grow and change with the organization, thereby avoiding the

execution paradox described in Part 1. Defining your system is the first step to managing it. Managing it is the next step to making it sustainable over the long term.

It would be easy if we were hardwired to obey the laws of physics, but we are not. We are a little God-like in our ability to have desires and the ability to pursue them. We are mini creators. Without some strategy for managing the increasing complexity of human interaction, chaos will eventually overtake your organization. It is just a question of when.

Design Requirements

To guide you in meeting this challenge, I suggest you design your system so that it meets the following five requirements.

1: Build It to Last

Years ago, this item would *not* have been at the top of my list, but experience has changed my thinking.

First, some backstory to my journey on this topic. We came across a little-known study published (Hendricks and Singhal, "Don't Count TQM Out," *Quality Progress* April 1999, repeated in 2012: Guoqiang Peter Zhang, Yusen Xia, *Production and Operations Management* Vol 22, No.1 Jan–Feb 2013) that crystalized something we were seeing in the field with clients.

The study's purpose was to determine whether organizations that used a systematic approach to managing their businesses performed better. The study covered ten years and used public company financial data for benchmarking results.

Study Methods

- Six hundred companies that implemented a holistic system were compared to six hundred companies in the same industry that did not implement a system.
- Analysts tracked performance for five years before and five years after implementation.
- Organizations from fifty industries worldwide were included.
- These six hundred companies implemented over one hundred different management/quality models.

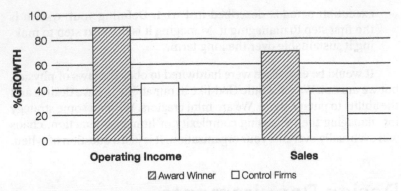

FIGURE 7.1 Growth of award winners versus control firm.

Findings

The six hundred organizations that fully implemented a system group grew sales 100% and earnings 90% faster than the six hundred companies that did not implement it. (See Figure 7.1.)

The brand of the "system" (model) implemented did not affect the results. Over one hundred different models were used.

Implementers in all industries, sizes, and countries outperformed non-implementors.

> There was one takeaway that forever changed my thinking. It was the fact that the management model did not influence the results. How well the system was implemented is what mattered most.

There was one takeaway that forever changed my thinking. It was the fact that the management model did not influence the results. How well the system was implemented is what mattered most.

In retrospect, it shouldn't have surprised me because I had often told people that your diet did not matter; it was following the one you chose. I realized that the principle of following the "model" is everywhere in the Bible. A pointed statements is made by the apostle John's challenging followers of Christ:

> And by this we know that we have come to know him, if we keep (follow) his commandments. Whoever says "I know him" but does not keep his commandments is a liar, and the truth is not in him.
>
> *I John 2*

In other places, the Bible refers to "overcoming," "reaping what you sow," "bearing fruit," and "abiding" They all reinforce the principle that the proof of what we believe manifests in our actions. Jesus, in my paraphrase, says, "Either follow me or don't, but don't pretend."

The application of this principle in building your system is that the overarching requirement for your system is that the practices chosen are implemented in a way that lasts.

> ...the overarching requirement for your system is that the practices chosen are implemented in a way that lasts.

As you pursue the remaining checklist items, ask yourself, "How can I sustain this behavior in my team?" It is the same as getting people to go to the gym or drink more water and keep doing it, week in, week out, year in, year out. Build great habits, and stick with them.

2: Choose Best Practices that Are Vital

What best practices will help the most? This was a question my research team began exploring. We found an abundance of ideas from thought leaders, including Michael Porter, W. Edwards Deming, Peter Drucker, Kurt Lewin, Stephen Covey, Peter Senge, Robert Kaplan, Jim Collins, Ram Charan, Patrick Lencioni, and many more.

We also found outcome-based models that show what management systems should achieve. But they do no prescribe how. Examples are the US-based Malcolm Baldrige Quality Award, the European Foundation for Quality Management, and various quality management models.

To guide you in your thinking, we have distilled those ideas into a vital few (six) themes, each of which is covered in its own chapter. These chapters identify many questions for you to consider what you want from your system.

In the Weight Watchers example, this is the equivalent of picking the diet program you want to follow. Most will work if you follow them.

3: Make the System Fit the Work

For any system to last, it has to fit how people work. It should fit how individuals interact with their leader and the team members who depend on them.

It should use the absolute minimum amount of control necessary to allow people to stay aligned effectively. I find the air traffic control system instructive. In 2019 there were thirty-nine million flights worldwide, which is over one hundred thousand per day. (Source: 45+ Air Travel Statistics [2022] SeedScientific. https://seedscientific.com/air-travel-statistics.)

> It [a system] should use the absolute minimum amount of control necessary to allow people to stay aligned effectively.

Air traffic control illustrates the power of a simple system handling great complexity. Flights are controlled by flight number, departure location and time, arrival location and time, and a flight plan addressing altitude. The system is simple and works amazingly well.

We notice three work models that people fall within. And if you force people into a model that doesn't fit, they simply quit following the system.

> If you force people into a model that doesn't fit, they simply quit following the system.

The three models with our nicknames follow.

- Freedom model (natural garden);
- Agility model (football team);
- Precision model (orchestra).

These are listed in the order of the increasing coordination interdependencies needed to be effective for the mission of the department they belong to.

Let's explore each in order.

The Freedom Model: Natural Garden   This model is for people who don't need a lot of day-to-day coordination with their leader and team to be effective.

The natural garden (Figure 7.2) represents the "you bloom where you are planted" type of culture. One example of this might be individuals doing research that is not subject to detailed planning. Start-ups can fall in this mode as well. You have a small group of people driving and innovating rapidly, and learning is the primary focus, not coordinated action. The fruit of this work should eventually result in products or services that must be implemented using more coordination.

Work that is highly repetitive is another example. People in those roles work without lots of formal controls. An example might be the accounting function for processing payroll, payables, or month-end closing and reporting.

Sometimes departments have similar workstyles and sometimes quite diverse. Identifying the right coordination model has to consider that diversity.

The next model requires more coordination among people on the team.

FIGURE 7.2   The freedom model.
Source: JACLOU-DL/Pixabay.

The Agility Model: Football Team Some work requires higher adaptability to everyday situations, which in turn requires close coordination among the team to stay aligned. There is a mutual interdependency to make this work.

The American football team model is a good analogy (see Figure 7.3). A team plan is required for the season since it affects player personnel. Then, a game plan is required for the next game. That plan considers the strengths and weaknesses of the opponent relative to the team's capability.

The team huddles, and a play is called. At the line of scrimmage, the quarterback may change the play if the situation requires it. Everyone has to listen and knows what to do.

After the play starts, individual players must "read" their opponent's behavior and adjust immediately. This requires skill by the individual player. Some plays work, and some don't. You go back to the huddle and call the next play, sharing what you learned.

Sometimes coaches make adjustments from the sidelines or the press box. Bigger adjustments occur at the quarter breaks and half-time. Individuals with specific skills must play their role. But on a

FIGURE 7.3 The agility model.

> You can't coach for this. Smart people read the situation and act because they know the bigger goal is to win.

broken play, anyone may be called to do something outside their role. You can't coach for this. Smart people read the situation and act because they know the bigger goal is to win.

There may be a debate in the huddle about the next play, but once the play is called, no one can do their own thing. There is more individualism in the way players respond to surprises as the play unfolds. Regardless of individual performance, everyone either wins or loses as a team.

Individuals need metrics to monitor how well they are delivering on their responsibilities. This feedback guides training priorities. This involves handheld devices for people working in the field or wall monitors for people working on the floor. Information has to deal with short-term needs and longer-term trends to identify areas of improvement.

The next model requires extreme precision and coordination.

The Precision Model: Orchestra An orchestra is the opposite of a natural garden. It takes extreme coordination. People willingly give up freedom to do something together that they could never do alone. And they experience an excellence and joy that can be attained no other way.

> People willingly give up freedom to do something together that they could never do alone.

An orchestra's precision (Figure 7.4) requires dozens of people to play every note at the right time and in the right way. Wow!

The marvel does not stop there. The orchestra includes many types of instruments, which represent centuries of craftsmanship. People who have rehearsed and developed their skills for decades assemble into assigned seats. The hall they play in is crafted for acoustics. And don't forget the genius of the composer. It is difficult to overstate the magnificence of all these pieces fitting together around a common purpose.

FIGURE 7.4   The precision model.
Source: Martin Good/Shutterstock.com.

> But most things we cannot achieve unless we give up individual freedom to achieve something beyond ourselves.

As mentioned before, this confronts our human design. We have strong desires and a mind of our own. But most things we cannot achieve unless we give up individual freedom to achieve something beyond ourselves

Helping people apply this trade-off is a daunting leadership challenge. It reminds me of a letter Paul wrote to the Church at Corinth where he was instructing them on the very idea that even though they were individuals, they were also part of a local church (the orchestra), and they needed to understand the trade-off we describe. When he speaks of the body, he is referring to the local church.

> *For the body does not consist of one member but of many. If the foot should say, "Because I am not a hand, I do not belong to the body," that would not make it any less a part of the body.*

And if the ear should say, "Because I am not an eye, I do not belong to the body," that would not make it any less a part of the body. If the whole body were an eye, where would be the sense of hearing? If the whole body were an ear, where would be the sense of smell?

Paul starts by explaining that each person has a different role but the same worth. The body needs you.

But as it is, God arranged the members in the body, each one of them, as he chose. If all were a single member, where would the body be? As it is, there are many parts, yet one body. The eye cannot say to the hand, "I have no need of you," nor again the head to the feet, "I have no need of you." On the contrary, the parts of the body that seem to be weaker are indispensable, and on those parts of the body that we think less honorable we bestow the greater honor, and our unpresentable parts are treated with greater modesty, which our more presentable parts do not require. But God has so composed the body, giving greater honor to the part that lacked it, that there may be no division in the body, but that the members may have the same care for one another.

Paul then challenges them to accept the leader's authority (God in this case) and their assignment. And he goes on to challenge their attitudes about the other roles in the group. If one member suffers, all suffer; if one member is honored, all rejoice.

> Since you are no longer just individuals but part of something bigger, you share in the result, whether suffering or rejoicing. We rise and fall together.

Paul finishes by reminding them of the most important truth of all. Since you are no longer just individuals but part of something bigger, you share in the result, whether suffering or rejoicing. We rise and fall together.

Remember that as you design your "system," the most important part of the system is to facilitate people working together toward a shared purpose. It is interesting that the very next part of Paul's letter is called the "love" chapter. I bet most of you have heard parts of this chapter quoted at weddings. It starts with, "If I speak with tongues of men and angels and do not have love, I have become a noisy gong or a clanging cymbal." Does it sound familiar?

I won't repeat it here, but this chapter was never intended for weddings; it explains how people working together to build the Church should treat each other. In the Bible, the binding force that holds people together is love—caring deeply about what is best for those around us. (See Chapter 14.)

We have covered a spectrum of minimal coordination of the garden model to the extreme coordination of the orchestra model. And in the middle is the football model, which has elements of both, lots of freedom with periods of tight coordination.

Let's move on to how to approach learning.

4: Integrate Learning with Doing

The set of best practices you choose should become the primary blueprint for your leadership development for two reasons.

First, in the ocean of training options, it prioritizes which skills are most important to develop for your particular organization.

Second, it creates a standard so that everyone is trained in the same model. Getting everyone using the same language and model facilitates better communication and faster learning.

> Another aim of your development and training strategy should be to train just in time, as leaders need it. We all learn faster by doing.

Another aim of your development and training strategy should be to train just in time, as leaders need it. We all learn faster by doing. Large block training in workshops guarantees you overload people with content they won't apply for a long time. As a result, application and subsequent mastery will be slower.

One of the best practices we advocate is that each leader learns to build a team development plan with each of their direct reports. This is covered in Chapter 13 and promotes a continuous learning culture.

The heart of your system is people, not technology. Whatever training approach you choose, it should provide continual reinforcement. As the organization grows, the capabilities of individuals have to grow too. Remember the skills deception in the previous chapter?

The overall aim is to grow capability faster than the organization's complexity grows. Otherwise, the execution paradox (Chapter 6) overtakes you.

5: Right Info at the Right Time

There was a time when I referred to some organizations as "high tech." Today that is a meaningless phrase. It is like calling humans "oxygen breathers." If you are alive, you are breathing oxygen. If you are in business, you are a high-tech business.

> If you are alive, you are breathing oxygen. If you are in business, you are a high-tech business.

When building your leadership system, you must have a technology strategy. You are "swimming in technology already," you say. I believe it. Most organizations are swimming in technology in every department they have.

> ...your leadership system has a different purpose than any of these systems. Its role is to equip leaders to be data-driven in their decision-making, integrating information from all key sources.

However, your leadership system has a different purpose than any of these systems. Its role is to equip leaders to be data-driven in their decision-making, integrating information from all key sources.

The system has to view everyone as a leader of something. And it must be clear about what that is and provide individualized information so that people can see both short-term and long-term issues to address.

Getting the right information to the right person at the right time is a science and an art form. It is not a project; it is an ongoing process that requires constant attention from every leader. They must listen, mentor, and adjust as they pay attention to their team's work. They have to protect people from too much information since systems and data have proliferated.

The good news is that business intelligence technologies are advancing rapidly. And so are the integration standards that make them more practical and cost-effective. But these technologies are only as effective as the leaders using them.

Final Caution on Your System

A disclaimer: no one can put into a system all aspects of successful leadership. But there are principles that decades of experience have found to be helpful. Is a system that facilitates managerial best practices necessary? Yes. Is it sufficient for business success? No. People must come first, and we focus on that in Part 3.

Peter Senge reinforces the same idea in his book about building learning organizations.

> Is a system that facilitates managerial best practices necessary? Yes. Is it sufficient for business success? No.

Vision without "systems thinking" ends up painting lovely pictures of the future with no deep understanding of the forces that must be mastered to move from here to there

Peter Senge, The Fifth Discipline

> You can't overcome chaos with words; you overcome it with purposeful action. Without purpose, actions just contribute to more chaos. Without action, chaos wins.

As a final thought about your system, I remind you that you can't overcome chaos with words; you overcome it with purposeful action. Without purpose, actions just contribute to more chaos. Without action, chaos wins.

1 Corinthians 12

In the next chapter, we'll explore vision formation. Be prepared for a lot of questions that only you can answer.

Takeaways

- For an organization to scale, some sort of leadership system has to be deployed. The system has to facilitate communication and growth in capability of the leadership on a continuing basis.
- Different work requires different leadership models. Three general models are:
  - Natural garden, which is for high creativity and low coordination overhead;
  - American football, which has a game plan but requires dynamic play calling and individual player adaptation to the play.
  - Orchestra, which is for extreme precision;
- It does not matter nearly as much what system you use but that you have a system that *is* used.

CHAPTER 8

Set Vision

Write down this vision; clearly inscribe it on tablets so one may easily read it.

Habakkuk 2, CSB

The battle against chaos starts with defining purpose. This chapter describes the basics of setting vision for any organization unit, whether at the enterprise or department level.

Setting vision is on everyone's leadership checklist. However, the result is often too vague to guide resource allocation in a way that gets results. A world with too many opportunities to pursue is just another form of chaos. The purpose of setting a clear vision is to bring focus to what problems you want to solve so that you can ignore the rest. As Michael Porter says, "The essence of strategy is deciding what not to do."

The Bible is full of examples of the use of vision by

> The battle against chaos starts with defining purpose.

> The purpose of setting a clear vision is to bring focus to what problems you want to solve so that you can ignore the rest.

leaders and God Himself. Vision aligns people around a shared purpose; the lack of vision causes chaos. Proverbs 29:18 states it this way: "When there's no vision, the people get out of control...."

One test of good visioning is that everyone understands the vision and relates their responsibilities to it. Another test is whether the vision provides the clarity for people to know how to invest their time. A clear path to increased chaos is "biting off more than you can chew."

1. Start with the "Why"

People not only *want* to know why; they *need* to know why.

It is the core of our design. Everything starts with the motivation and desire part of our being. Leaders must answer the why questions to engage the hearts and minds of those around us.

Your leadership system must encourage leaders to define the organization's mission and values. The result is a clear statement about why the organization exists and what its character is. The strategy changes periodically, and the tactics change continually, but the mission and values provide transcending stability.

> I noticed in my own organizations that the more we emphasize mission and values in the recruiting process, the more we attract people who align with us.

I noticed in my own organizations that the more we emphasize mission and values in the recruiting process, the more we attract people who align with us. Our mission is to "improve leader effectiveness," and our values are "honoring God, excellence, and lasting relationships." These few words encapsulate why we exist and what is important to us.

This kind of clarity draws like-minded people who expect us to follow them. Instead of new hires "diluting" the culture, they strengthen it. Purpose is powerful, and it compounds.

Now for a few thoughts on how to craft mission.

Mission

Mission explains why an organization exists—its purpose, which should be long-lasting. TED (talk) mission is to "spread ideas." In only two words they convey why they exist and cast an enduring focus that seems like it could last forever.

A friend once told me that "people don't want to work for a company that *has* a mission but for a company that is *on* a mission." When you read "spread ideas," doesn't it make you want to join such an organization?

As you establish your approach for setting and managing the mission, consider the following.

Mission Checklist

☐ Is your mission authentic? Does it reflect the why behind the organization?

☐ Is it enduring? Will this purpose be valid for twenty-five years or longer?

☐ Is it memorable? Is it simple enough to be powerful? Can everyone in the organization state it without thinking?

☐ Do you live the mission? Is it central to decision-making? Is it clear to everyone that this purpose drives the organization? Do you just *have* a mission, or are you *on* a mission?

☐ Do you hold people accountable individually to the mission? Is it part of your feedback and review process?

☐ Do you emphasize the mission in recruiting? Is it attracting like-minded people who strengthen the commitment to the mission? Or is growth weakening your culture?

☐ Do you have systematic ways of renewing focus on the mission? Have you defined ways of helping people connect the dots on fresh internal stories that illustrate the value and meaning of the mission? Would Walt Disney think that the current Disney is living his original mission?

> Do you just *have* a mission, or are you *on* a mission?

Examples

- National Geographic

    The National Geographic Society uses the power of science, exploration, education, and storytelling to illuminate and protect the wonder of our world.

- MailChimp

    Send better email. We help millions of customers to find their audience, engage their clients, and build their brands.

- Hope Initiative Alliance

    Hope Initiative Alliance works together with our partners to improve the quality of life of marginalized people globally.

    Let's move from "why" to the character of the organization—its values.

Values

Those things that you hold as more important than short-term success are your values.

Values should be a character standard for the organization—the nonnegotiable traits that everyone is expected to aspire to embody.

> Those things that you hold as more important than short-term success are your values.

These items are more important than economic success. People are not perfect and will make mistakes, but values must be real and affect behavior and decision-making.

Peter Senge tells a powerful story in *The Fifth Discipline* that shows what it means for people to struggle to understand what values mean in the day-to-day decisions. This story picks up in a planning session discussing what they mean by "honesty and forthrightness."

> *The management team had developed a vision they were getting excited about, when one of the senior salespeople commented offhandedly, "Of course, we don't mean that we'll be honest with our customers." The entire process ground to a halt. The group reconsidered what they meant by*

"commitment to honesty and forthrightness in all commu-
nications."
    The president broke the silence by stating, "Yes. For me,
this means being completely honest with our customers." The
salesperson responded, "If we do, we'll lose 30 percent of our
bookings next month. In this business, none of our competi-
tors are honest when they tell a customer when a new com-
puter system will arrive. If we tell the truth, our delivery times
will be 50 percent longer than what customers believe they get
from our competitors."
    "I don't care," was the president's response. "I simply
don't want to be a part of an organization that sanctions
lying to our customers, our vendors or anyone else. Moreover,
I believe that, over time, we'll establish a reputation for reli-
ability with our customers that will win us more customers
than we'll lose."
    The exchange continued for more than an hour. At the
end, the group was together in support of telling the truth.
The salesperson knew that if the bookings dropped off in the
next month or two, the other members of the team would not
come screaming for his head. And he and the rest had begun
to develop a vision of building a new reputation for honesty
and reliability among their customers.
    Peter Senge, The Fifth Discipline: Art and Practice of the
Learning Organization. *Random House Business Books, 1992.*

Whereas mission answers the question of "why" an organization exists, values speak to the character or "personality" of the organization. Experience teaches that to cope with a rapidly changing
world, organizations must decide on those things that won't change.
These become the found-
ation upon which endur-
ing success is built. Shared
values should be just as
enduring as the mission
and are just as important, if
not more so.
    This story demonstra-
tes courage and conviction.
It shows what kind of organization they want to spend

> Experience teaches
> that to cope with a
> rapidly changing world,
> organizations must
> decide on those things
> that won't change.

their lives in. This kind of leadership leads to greater loyalty, higher trust, and better performance.

The following checklist and the examples provide ideas for the habits your leadership system should encourage for answering the "why" question.

Values Checklist

☐ Are the values important to you? Do they evoke passion? Is it clear when they are violated, as in the preceding story? Are they more important than your biggest customer or a valuable employee?

☐ Are they clear and memorable? People can't remember 10 values. Stick to three max.

☐ Are they enduring? Will they be valid for twenty or thirty years?

☐ Do you hold people accountable to the organization's values? Is it part of your feedback and review process?

☐ Do you emphasize the mission in recruiting? Is it attracting like-minded people who live these values? Or is the culture weakened as you grow?

☐ Do you have systematic ways of renewing focus on the values? Have you defined ways of helping people connect the dots on fresh internal stories that illustrate the value and meaning of the mission.

Examples

Following are examples of the kinds of values I hear organizations discussing.

- Honesty and integrity;
- Responsibility/accountability;
- Respect;
- Openness/transparency;
- Excellence;
- Customer-driven;
- Innovation;
- Equity/social justice/fairness;

- Artisanship;
- Quality;
- Action oriented.

The next step in answering the vision question is being clear about who your customers are and what they need.

2. Know Your Customers

Your customer is whoever you serve, whether inside or outside the organization. They pay the bill. In a nonprofit, it is those who need your services. Some departments, such as HR, accounting, and IT, serve internal customers.

Your leadership system should reinforce clarifying who the customer is and also promote the interaction required to know how well those needs are being met. Often, organizations talk about the need for customer focus. But the proof that it is difficult to deliver is how noticeable it is when you experience excellence as a customer. It is rare enough that it stands out. Think about phone support experiences or fast-food experiences. Some are great; some are not. You get the idea.

As you establish your approach for maintaining a focus on knowing your customer, refer to the following checklist.

Know Your Customer Checklist

☐ Are you hiring people who care about customers? Do they want more from their job than a paycheck? You can train people on customer best practices, but you can't make them care.

> You can train people on customer best practices, but you can't make them care.

☐ Is it clear to everyone what business the organization is in? The services you will and will not provide?

☐ Does everyone understand what markets (customer segments) you are targeting? (See Figure 8.1.)

Market Definition

Market Requirement	Yuppie Segment	Young Family Segment	Empty Nest Segment
Price Sensitive	Medium	Medium	Low
Safety	Low	High	Medium
Mileage	Low	Medium	High
Sporty Style	High	Low	Medium
4+ Seating	Low	High	Medium

Determines what you "build"

FIGURE 8.1   Market definition.
Source: LeadFirst.ai

☐ Is there a process for updating and communicating changes in customer targeting?

☐ Does your business intelligence strategy include ongoing feedback from customers? Is the information timely enough to catch issues early? Daily? Weekly? Quarterly? Is this information readily available to everyone in the organization that could affect the results?

☐ Do you understand your customer's alternatives and how well you compare? Is there information available to educate employees on competitors and their strengths relative to yours? (See Figure 8.2.) And how does that relate to strategy?

☐ Is customer focus visible in employee feedback and reviews? Are the principles above applied to internal customers, too? Does everyone know what their internal customer need? Are you tracking their satisfaction?

☐ Are internal customers free to choose outside alternatives if they are not getting what they need? Is there a mindset of having to earn the business of internal customers?

☐ Do you have systematic ways of building a client-driven culture? Are their success stories shared regularly that remind people to be proactive instead of reactive?

Competitive Analysis

Competitive Strengths	Our Company	Competitor A	Competitor B
Brand	Low	High	Low
Cost (scale)	Medium	High	Medium
Distribution	Medium	High	Medium
Innovation	High	Low	Medium
Service	High	Medium	Medium

FIGURE 8.2 Competitive analysis.
Source: LeadFirst.ai

After getting clarity of who your customers are and their needs, the next step in visioning is deciding how the organization will establish a sustainable difference.

3. Quantify What You're Best At

The ability to build and sustain a product or service offering that differs from that of rivals, and differs in ways that are important to customers, is the foundation of a healthy business.

For a strategic difference to be sustainable, the detailed activities required to deliver it must be different than those of your competitors. The offerings and activities must force competitors to maintain their current strategic position or attack yours.

> For a strategic difference to be sustainable, the detailed activities required to deliver it must be different than those of your competitors.

A client I worked with positioned themselves as a full-service marketing firm. They wanted to target clients that would use the company as a one-stop shop for their marketing needs. In today's world, this requires public relations, social media, search engine optimization, outbound email, graphic design, website development, content creation, and digital advertising. Also required is account and project management to coordinate all these services.

"Full-service" positioned the firm against the specialty houses focusing on website building or email campaigns. So the strategic position was clear and differentiable. However, the second part of the positioning strategy is to assure that the activities (investments) of the organization support and deliver on the strategic position. As we probed the team's depth of expertise, we found a few seasoned people had broad expertise. They could talk a good game in closing a sale, but they had no bench strength to deliver promises.

This kind of misalignment creates chaos in the organization. After the sale, as projects progressed, the few people with expertise became overloaded. Clients were unhappy with missed commitments, and the operation became reactive to unhappy customers.

The point of crafting a vision is to make sure that your organization knows what it is promising. This is a prerequisite for an investment strategy for delivering it. This lack of clarity may work with a small team but as specialization increases, coordination and communication make alignment impossible.

One way to scale the aligning power of your competitive advantage is to attach a single measure that encapsulates that value-add. A single measure is difficult to define, but it is unmatched in the alignment guidance for the rest of the organization.

> A single measure is difficult to define, but it is unmatched in the alignment guidance for the rest of the organization.

For example, to figure out the measure of "full-service" positioning, ask what benefit "full service" brings the customer. "Time to solution" might be high value for some clients. If that were your choice, then define that metric. The rest of the organization can then align around improving that number. Without that clarity, everyone is optimizing for their view of "full service," and you end up being excellent at nothing.

Your investments make your value-add sustainable. If this firm had built the infrastructure to be full service, then a boutique shop could not compete for clients who want that service. In reverse, if someone just wanted SEO optimization and nothing else, the boutique firm would have the advantage over the full-service firm in terms of expertise and cost.

Your leadership system should encourage a clear definition of a measurable strategic position for the organization to grow and stay aligned with the promises made to customers.

Best At Checklist

☐ In three to five words can you answer the question: "What you want to be best at?" "Full-service marketing," "biggest selection of books," "lowest priced foods," "premium service auto repair"? Does everyone understand it?

☐ Do you have a primary measure for your difference? For example, which of the following positioning statements will align behavior in a health care organization the best?

   o "Best at Patient Service."

   o "Best at Patient Service with 95% visit completion within forty-eight hours from request."

☐ Is your chosen area of differentiation sustainable? Are you able to make the investments to keep ahead? If not, narrow your focus until you meet or beat your promises.

☐ Is the distinction between "operational efficiency" and strategic position clear? As Michael Porter says, operational efficiency involves "constant change, flexibility, and best practices," but strategy "demands discipline, continuity; its enemies are distraction and compromise."

☐ Are people accountable for plan reviews and individual feedback to know and align to the strategic position?

Now to envision how growth will occur.

4. Quantify "Growth" Vision

Laying out a growth strategy is the last step in creating a vision that your team can align around. In this step, you picture the organization seven to ten years in the future. It should be far enough in the future that it's not a plan but a vision.

Most organizations grow in some combination of the following four dimensions:

- Product/service offering;
- Demographic markets such as age, profession, gender, and ethnicity;
- Distribution channels, such as store-front retail, online, and distributors;
- Geographic markets such as regions of the world, countries, or localities.

> It translates the decisions in the previous three steps into something much more concrete and less subject to interpretation error by others.

Quantifying long-term vision in terms of these four dimensions clears up a great deal of misalignment in strategy. It translates the decisions in the previous three steps into something much more concrete and less subject to interpretation error by others.

When coaching organizations, I've found that teams often think they are on the same page on the vision based on the prior steps, and they go to complete this step and realize they are not on the same page at all.

One small but growing consulting firm client in Colorado Springs got to this point in their planning session, where I asked what they thought the organization should aim for in terms of growth over the next ten years. The answers varied from $250 million to $500 million. The leader was shocked. These people had worked together for years and yet had very different ideas about the future and didn't know it. You can't execute any plan with this lack of clarity.

Growth Vision Checklist

☐ Do you have a ten-year growth vision? Considering historical, industry, and competitive growth rates, how fast would you like to grow over the next ten years? (This isn't about precision but vision casting.)

☐ What are the past five year sales for major products/services? What would you like them to be in ten years? Are you adding new products and phasing out old ones?

☐ What are the sources of sales in terms of markets served (types of customers)? What would you like them to be in ten years? Are you adding new markets and phasing out old ones?

☐ What are the sources of sales in terms of channels of distribution (delivery models such as distributors, retail, or online)? What would you like them to be in ten years? Are you adding new channels and phasing out old ones?

☐ What are the sources of sales in terms of geographies served? What would you like them to be in ten years? Are you adding new geographies and phasing out old ones?

☐ Do you have ways of engaging *everyone* in this vision? Can every department leader explain it?

☐ Are there feedback channels for potential barriers to the vision? Do people understand the difference between a vision and a plan? Are there items of concern or fear?

Example Growth Vision

Figure 8.3 shows a simple illustration of how a growth strategy might appear in a spreadsheet format. You would have more history and some intervening years leading up to the 10-year vision, but the essence of the idea is to document how much growth you want and how you will achieve that growth.

In concluding our discussion on vision, please recall that the opposite of chaos is purpose. The first responsibility of a leader is to figure out how to order chaos to serve a chosen purpose. Vision is the "true north" indicator around which everyone in the organization can align.

Growth Strategy	Today	10-Year Vision	Growth
Products/Services (what you sell)			
Product A	$49m	$70m	$70m
Product B	$1m	$100m	$100m
Markets (who you sell to)			
Gen X	25m	20m	$5m
Gen Z	25m	150m	$125m
Channels (how you sell/deliver)			

FIGURE 8.3   Growth strategy.
Source: LeadFirst.ai

Takeaways

- Chaos is overcome with purpose. Clear vision is the mandatory starting point for organization performance.

- Mission and values tend to get diluted with growth. You system of leadership has to offset this tendency.

- Growth exposes organizations to increasing market and product opportunities. Clarity of target customers and needs is essential to maintain alignment.

- Sustainability of organization success depends on understanding the strategy for differentiation. What is this organization going to excel at? Without this clarity, everyday decision-making by the people in the trenches will be defocused.

- Leaders need to paint a vision of the long-term future in quantified terms. What markets, channels of distribution, product lines, geographies? It is the quantification that cuts through all the jargon and helps the front lines understand direction. The numbers do not need to be accurate time-wise, just directionally sound.

CHAPTER 9

Prioritize Change

For which of you, desiring to build a tower, does not first sit down and count the cost, whether he has enough to complete it?

Luke 14

Dreaming about what we want is not enough. Like the quote above suggests, it requires "sitting down" and thinking about your resources and how to best use them.

Remember when we discussed that sequence matters? Your leadership system has to recognize that setting change priorities is sequenced after vision formation. Otherwise, change is not purposeful. It also means that the order you complete change is critical. How should the changes that need to be made be sequenced?

This chapter identifies how to create a change road map that supports the strategy. If you don't change fast enough, you fall behind. That leads to chaos. If you change too quickly, you disrupt daily

> If you don't change fast enough, you fall behind. That leads to chaos. If you change too quickly, you disrupt daily operations.

operations and create a different type of chaos. How you manage change matters.

Whether focused on total organization strategy or for an individual department, the role of the leader is to understand what needs to change and how fast. Change is costly and stressful, so you only want to introduce change that drives the vision.

1. Set Change Pace

Considering long-term vision, leaders should specify how fast to move toward the vision. Where do you need to be in two years, five years, seven years? Remember, the vision lays out long-term destination, and the change strategy is a road map for getting there. Operating plans are more detailed and cover the next couple of years. Think of pace-setting as defining the first steps toward the vision. And they become targets in the operating plans.

> We recommend setting targets two years beyond the fiscal year that you are in. There can be a significant lead time between change and seeing the results.

We recommend setting targets two years beyond the fiscal year that you are in. There can be a significant lead time between change and seeing the results. If you want specific results in two years, people need to work into next year's plan how that will happen.

Failure to think a couple of years ahead is a major source of chaos. The alternative is a last-minute rush, which disrupts operations and creates stress, firefighting, and loss of confidence in leadership.

There are always unforeseen circumstances that require rapid adjustments to this road map and to operating plans. It takes wise leadership to know when to make adjustments and when to hold the line. Like the old fable about the boy "who cried wolf," if you are in revision mode constantly, something is wrong, and people will burn out and lose faith in leadership.

Learning to Embrace Constraints

When setting the change in pace consider how to embrace constraints. From childhood on, we grow up fighting limitations that constrain us. Yet there are many historical examples where severe constraints (problems) provided a setting that incubated great creative thinking. Sometimes, "necessity is the mother of invention."

> Yet there are many historical examples where severe constraints (problems) provided a setting that incubated great creative thinking. Sometimes, "necessity is the mother of invention."

One great faith lesson is the story of Gideon in the Bible. This story takes place about 3,500 years ago. God called Gideon to become a leader in a chaotic time. He had no experience and needed to raise an army. And when he requested men to join an army to fight their enemies, over 30,000 men showed up. God told Gideon it was way too many people. In victory, he and his people would think they won because of their large army. God instructed Gideon to reduce the army's size to three hundred, about 1% of what he started with.

Being forced to face a large enemy with a small force was designed by God to test whether Gideon trusted in God's direction. It sounds easy when you read the story, but in reality, it would likely stretch you beyond your own limitations.

Take as another example the Apollo 13 mission. When, due to an explosion three astronauts were stranded half-way to the moon, the men's survival was unlikely. Yet NASA engineers on the ground accepted the limitations and used materials on board in a truly innovative way to save the three men's lives. In this situation, fighting the constraints would have wasted precious time.

> Confusing as it may seem, leaders must cope with the conflict of attempting to plan and realizing that plans are never right.

Confusing as it may seem, leaders must cope with

the conflict of attempting to plan and realizing that plans are never right. The real value of planning is building into your team a shared understanding of what you are trying to accomplish. That understanding makes the organization more resilient when unexpected change comes.

Change Pace Checklist

☐ Do you have a metric model for your organization that allows you to understand the *relationships* among key metrics? If you want sales to be x in two years, what leads are needed next year? If you want customer retention improved from x to y in two years, how will that affect sales?

☐ Does your metric model connect people to see the strategy? Do they lead them to do the right things today? Most metrics are both leading and lagging, depending on who is looking at them. Sales are a leading indicator of profitability. But it is a lagging indicator of the number of leads. This metric architecture helps align day-to-day activities to the vision.

☐ Are metric targets supported by trended history, so gaps between targets and trends are clear? If growth in territory X has been 10% per year for the last few years, but you want it to be 20% a year from now, is that gap clear? Making the gap clear prompts the alignment question: How will that happen?

☐ Have you identified the vital few (three to five) metrics that drive most of the success for the organization, so people know what to focus on?

☐ Do you have an approach for setting top-down targets to give people something to shoot for? Are there clear feedback loops to revise those targets according to bottom-up planning? Is there a way to differentiate between nonnegotiable and adjustable targets? Are there too many rigid targets that set up the organization for failure? Which is vital and which is not?

> Have you identified the vital few (three to five) metrics that drive most of the success for the organization?

After setting near-term targets that clarify growth rates, move on to defining key change initiatives.

2. Charter Vital Projects

In this step, you identify the strategic projects needed to close the gap between targets and trends (see Figure 9.1). The idea is to identify the major changes needed, not to overwhelm with detail. At the organizational level, these can be multi-year change initiatives, for example, creating a new product line, implementing a new ERP system, or opening a new geographical market.

At the department level, this could be an annual project that will require a lot of cooperation among the team members. Examples could be upgrade the CRM system in marketing or expand space in an existing health care facility.

A warning is reflected in the checklist. Most organizations are not very good at chartering projects, sequencing them, and resourcing them. This checklist and the one in the next chapter, related to projects, expose the weaknesses.

Identify The Gaps

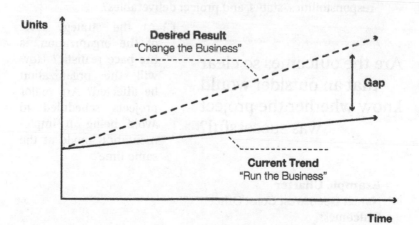

FIGURE 9.1   Closing the gap.
Source: LeadFirst.ai

Charter Vital Projects Checklist

☐ Do you have projects explaining how the gaps in *critical* metrics will be closed?

☐ Do these projects have a clear charter? What are the specific, measurable outcomes that define success for the project? Are the outcomes so clear that an outsider would know whether the project was successful?

☐ Are constraints clear and prioritized? Do they incorporate schedule, resources, and scope? Which of these three constraints are most important? Least?

☐ Have you assessed the risk level? Has the organization (or project team) ever done this type of project before? Are new technologies involved? Large external dependencies? What impact does implementation have on operations? What happens if it is late?

☐ Is the project governance settled? Who is the sponsor? Who has *the skill and the time* to manage the project? Who will the project leader report to? How often?

☐ Is there a deadline for organizing the project? When will staffing be assigned? Is the first milestone of the project producing a project plan?

☐ Is there a tracking system that facilitates communicating responsibilities, status, and project deliverables?

☐ At the strategy level of the organization, is the pace realistic? How will the organization be affected? Are major projects scheduled to avoid being in implementation mode at the same time?

> Are the outcomes so clear that an outsider would know whether the project was successful?

Example Charter
Name: Open West Coast Office
Outcomes:

- Sales $10m first full year of operation
- Open by 9/1/xx for Christmas season

Project Manager: Anthony Jones
Constraints:

- Capital Budget $7m

Risks

- Availability of qualified people
- Local regulatory approval

After change priorities are clear, the next step is to free up resources by stopping lower priority projects.

3. Stop the Nonessential

One source of chaos is trying to do more than you have the resources to do. The inclination is to think you can squeeze it in. Sometimes yes, but most often no. If it's a critical project, it is better to drop lower-priority items.

> But most of the time, when an agenda item arrives, they can't agree on stopping anything.

The idea of stopping lower-priority work is initially appealing. In our experience people see "what to stop" on the planning agenda, their eyes light up and say something like, "Can't wait to get to that topic." But most of the time, when that agenda item arrives, they can't agree on stopping anything. Rarely has any organization ever mustered the will to do that.

As a CEO, I have been there. In a previous company, we had a large project that I should have stopped, but I couldn't let go. The more we invested in it, the more I felt I had to make it work. As a result, the business was at risk, and I had to lay off many friends. It was a hard lesson.

In contrast, there are many success stories. One of our clients in the construction industry anticipated a recession. Their leadership analyzed all their product lines and customers, and figured out that 20% of customers and products drove their profitability. They gradually phased out the rest. The result was amazing. While the industry was in desperate conditions for the next two years, they grew their business 50% and did not add one person to their payroll.

The deceptions we talked about in Chapter 6 are at work. It is difficult to stop doing lower-priority things, but the payoff for doing so is significant.

Stop the Nonessential Checklist

☐ Is there a focus on finding and stopping wasted activity? Are employees regularly asked to identify time wasters?

☐ Do people understand that stopping is not a failure but a success? Are people threatened by stopping wasted activities that are part of their work?

> Do people understand that stopping is not a failure but a success? Are people threatened by stopping wasted activities?

☐ Does your organization consistently review the importance of projects? Is there a rigorous prioritization process?

☐ Are the ongoing responsibilities of individuals defined with clarity and do they have supporting measures? Do those measures align with the organization's vision?

☐ When people identify misalignments, are they addressed promptly and with openness?

☐ When you stop things, is there a good plan for doing it? Does the plan consider the impact on internal and external stakeholders? Doing this right will reduce fear when the next item is identified.

At this stage, the vision and change road map are completed. It is now important to answer how everyone gets engaged with this strategy.

4. Connect People to Purpose

Do you have an intentional strategy for connecting people to the purpose of the organization—its mission, values, and vision? Success in engaging people's hearts and minds is a leadership mindset.

When Nehemiah was attempting to rebuild the walls of Jerusalem, a huge task in enemy territory with few resources, he gathered information about the size of the project at night so no one would see him. He put together a plan. Then he gathered the right people and explained the vision for the project. The response was, "Let us arise and build." "So they put their hands to the good work" (Nehemiah 2).

Do you, as a leader, see the importance of engaging people in the "why" behind the strategy—its vision and the changes that need to take place?

Doing this correctly is a tall order. It means more than casually reading or watching a video about the strategy. It requires thinking about its measures and how your department's strategy tie into the organization's strategy. It also means sitting down with every team member and explaining their job and why it matters. It means connecting in the mind of each individual why their work is important and how to best align with it.

> ## What engages you? When was the last time you got excited about something?

Is it worth it? To answer that question, think about your own life. How important is it to you to be doing work that matters? This is not a rhetorical question. What engages you? When was the last time you got excited about something? Not just a moment of excitement, such as a sport's big play, but the excitement that stirred you to do something that you wouldn't have done otherwise. Are you engaged in your work now? Is the organization's mission important to you?

Some people view work as just a means to an end. They need income to put food on the table, and that's it. Their deeper purpose comes from their family, hobbies, or something else. Others want their work to matter deeply. And it makes them miserable when they don't see the connection. Or they see the connection, but the organization is so dysfunctional that they feel like they can't win.

> It makes them miserable when they don't see the connection. Or they see the connection, but the organization is so dysfunctional that they feel like they can't win.

One premise of this book is that God equipped everyone to overcome chaos, giving everyone a powerful desire to win at something. Part of a leader's role is to help unlock that power, even when it's hidden.

I used to think the way to "connect people to purpose" was a presentation explaining the organization's strategy and maybe small group discussions. I now see this as a way of life for all leaders. Leaders should continually relate how what is happening today connects to the bigger picture.

This is not a new idea. When Moses was instructing the Israelites on how to train their children on basic truths, he said, "Repeat them again and again to your children. Talk about them when you are at home and when you are on the road, when you are going to bed and when you are getting up" (New Living Translation, Deuteronomy 6:7. https://biblehub.com/nlt/deuteronomy/6.htm).

Connect People to Purpose Checklist

☐ Are leaders trained on how to engage people with the vision? Are they held accountable for it in their feedback and reviews?

☐ Are employees expected to understand the vision and strategy? This is not just the leader's responsibility. Is this part of individual feedback and review?

☐ How do you handle employees who simply won't engage with the vision? Is this acceptable? Are you getting compliance or commitment?

☐ Is part of the company culture to talk about the vision and strategy in meetings and impromptu conversations? Are resources available explaining the strategy? Are there visible updates on progress toward the strategy (dashboards, reports)?

This completes the chapter on prioritizing change. In the next chapter, we will discuss how to keep running the business while trying to change it. Quite a balancing act.

Takeaways

- A road map that connects how to get from today to the vision helps keep the urgent from crowding out the important.
- A key leadership role is determining how fast change should occur: too slow and you fall behind competitively; too fast and current customer needs are sacrificed.
- Chartering is an essential skill that sets up change initiatives for success or failure. Charters must define what success means for this project.
- The ability to identify lower-priority activities and stop them intelligently frees up resource and reduces complexity to execute better. It is crucial viewing stopping as a success, not a failure.
- Plans are typically formed by a few people with multiple meetings and conversations that build up their understanding over time. The rest of the organization needs a well-thought-out way to transfer the meaning behind decisions to the rest of the organization.

CHAPTER 10

Balance Running and Changing

The plans of the diligent lead surely to abundance, but everyone who is hasty comes only to poverty.
Proverbs 21

At this stage, after strategy formation, leaders must cope with the most challenging aspect of organizational dynamics—balancing resources between short-term operating needs and long-term strategic needs.

> After strategy formation, leaders must cope with the most challenging aspect of organizational dynamics—balancing resources between short-term operating needs and long-term strategic needs.

Let's take another look at the Nehemiah wall-rebuilding project. Their approach was to break down this massive task into sections of walls assigned to specific families. They worked in parallel to complete the task quickly. Because their enemies were trying to stop them, some people were assigned to defense. Everyone carried a sword, and there was an agreed-upon communication process (a trumpet) to signal if an attack was underway so reinforcements would arrive quickly. They planned carefully on how to work together.

Your own approach depends on organization size. Typically you must align vertically through multiple layers, and you must align horizontally to coordinate across functions. This process is fraught with communication and coordination challenges. The difficulty increases because of the requirement to run the organization at the same time you are changing it. Running the business refers to the daily things people do to keep operations working.

> Typically you must align vertically through multiple layers, and you must align horizontally to coordinate across functions.

The daily flow of issues, surprises, and priorities will always try to crowd out important but less urgent items.

This is where understanding brain design help us. Daily activity feeds the routine midbrain functioning, where you have "done this before" and are working out of habit. People prefer to work in this zone especially when they are busy. They are more productive, and it is easier.

Change management requires people to step out of their habits and do something they haven't done before. This creates two issues: learning something new *and* the extra time required. In most organizations, if you ask people what amount of time they spend running the business, they say close to 100%.

> In most organizations, if you ask people what amount of time they spend running the business, they say close to 100%.

They think they don't have any capacity to do other things. And along comes someone who says we need to "implement this new system," or "upgrade this process," or "add this new product."

In Figure 10.1, the first two stacks on the left represent this situation. The first box is the amount of resources available.

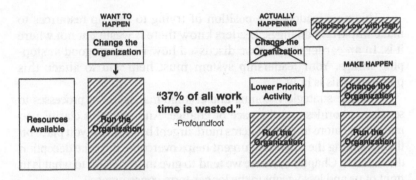

FIGURE 10.1   Running versus changing.

FIGURE 10.2   Wasted time.

Source: Adapted from How to identify wasted time and inefficiency—Clockify Blog.

> 31% of people report wasting one hour per day and an additional 26% report wasting two hours per day.

The second stack represents changes requested that don't appear to fit into the resources available.

Before accepting the premise that you do not have enough resources, it is important to remember that it is always true that some activities are not as important. A recent study by Salary.com (Figure 10.2) shows that 31% of people report wasting one hour per day and an additional 26% report wasting two hours per day.

This puts leaders in a position of trying to free up resources to make important changes. Leaders know there is waste but not where it is. In an earlier chapter, we discussed how we aren't good at stopping things. Your leadership system must help you to attack this problem. This is how.

You use strategic visioning and change management processes to set clear priorities and the pace of change. And with this clarity, you make these more important items more urgent by the focus you place on them. Making the important urgent helps overcome the time deception discussed in Chapter 6, where we tend to give more weight to what is in front of us and less weight to the longer-term consequences.

With a robust system of prioritization and accountability, you work on the higher-priority items first. The lower-priority items never get addressed. We have found that "displacing" waste is easier than trying to find it and stopping it.

> **"Displacing" waste is easier than trying to find it and stopping it.**

Stephen Covey popularized this displacement idea using the metaphor of putting the most important items (big rocks) into your "priorities bucket" first and letting the unimportant things (sand) fill in around it (Figure 10.3).

In contrast, if you allow the sand in first, it is difficult to get the top-priority items in the bucket. This analogy is just as helpful now as it was when he introduced it over twenty-five years ago.

> **A critical requirement of your leadership system is keeping the important things urgent so that they don't get pushed aside.**

Thus, a critical requirement of your leadership system is keeping the important things urgent so that they don't get pushed aside. Maintaining an aligned focus on the right priorities gets more difficult the larger the organization becomes. This is because the growth dynamics introduce hidden complexity that dilutes communication, as discussed in the growth deception in Chapter 6.

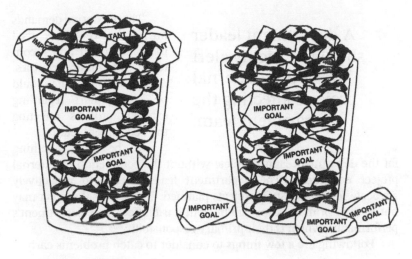

FIGURE 10.3   Big rocks.

In this chapter, we will focus on four best practices for running and changing the organization at the same time. The process described is for a single organization unit (division, department). All other units repeat this process, which is how it scales.

The first issue to address is resourcing important projects that originate *outside* the department.

1. Resource External Projects

Department staff spends most of its time on internal department priorities. For example, if you are in the engineering department, the team is spending its time gathering requirements and creating designs and specifications. As a result, that is where management time is focused.

However, some projects originate outside a department (strategic initiatives or other cross-functional projects). And they have a major impact on the department. These projects are often not well planned and create considerable disruption later. An example would be an IT project moving services to the cloud that could affect engineering mission-critical technologies. The engineering department needs to give attention to this project, though it is outside their responsibility.

> A department leader should be highly alert regarding external projects affecting the department team.

These external demands on internal resources need to be identified and reconciled with other priorities. A department leader should be highly alert regarding external projects affecting the department team.

To be clear, planning for the department is incomplete without the completion of external project definitions. The department leader needs to proactively advocate for getting such projects planned. That external project may not be their primary responsibility, but it *will* affect their department's performance, which *is* their primary responsibility.

Following are a few things to consider to catch problems early.

Resource External Projects Checklist

- ☐ Are projects assigned to a qualified project manager? Do they have the time to manage the project?

- ☐ Are project outcomes measurable? What vision metrics will it improve? By how much?

- ☐ Is there a staffing plan for the project that includes time commitment and duration?

- ☐ Is a date set for a project plan to be completed, identifying deliverables for at least the next quarter or two?

- ☐ Is a budget for the project (or at least the first phase) approved? Without an approved budget, the schedule is unpredictable.

- ☐ Is the risk profile of the project understood? Is this something the organization has experience with? Is the organization likely to manage this project well?

- ☐ Will there be an impact on the group during the project implementation, such as training or process changes?

☐ Has the department leader communicated the impact on their operations to their leader about this project?

☐ Is there a status reporting process for all projects?

Remember we talked about how important sequence is? Addressing the preceding questions sets up the next step, which is operational planning for a department team.

2. Plan as a Team

At this step, the leader of a department should know the strategic priorities coming from their own leader. This includes any key metrics and targets for those metrics that the department owns. Also, the impact of external projects should be clear.

The leader should model key metric performance to identify two-year metric target gaps to address in the plan. The leader should go into the department planning meeting with a clear draft picture of *what (not necessarily how)* the group needs to accomplish.

> The leader should go into the planning meeting with a clear draft picture of *what (not not necessarily how)* the group needs to accomplish.

By providing targets beyond the current year, activities needed this year to meet next year's targets are more likely to get done. Said another way, often, year one work lays the foundation for year two results, so it is important to get year two targets in view.

There are three main purposes for group planning:

• Increase understanding of the plan and how it fits into the strategy. Plans are never right for long. But planning gives people understanding and context to make better decisions, faster.

- Break into more detail the plans for meeting specific objectives. The leader thinks carefully about *what* needs to be achieved, and the person(s) assigned figures out how.
- Verify that the "what" part of the plan is correct. Often exploring *how* to do something, affects the *what* definition. Think of it as a top-down flow of objectives with detailed bottom-up planning that confirms the objectives can be met.

> Plans are never right for long. But planning gives people understanding and context to make better decisions, faster.

The following checklist provides guidance on how to achieve these three purposes.

Plan as a Team Checklist

☐ Are the responsibilities for the department listed? These typically appear in the manager's job description.

☐ Are two-year targets identified for each responsibility?

☐ Is there a "vision" target for each ongoing responsibility? Are best practices researched and used to set vision targets?

(For example, let's say you have the following scenario:

Industry average COGS is	35%
Your COGS is running	40%
Long-term vision target	33% (better than industry average)
Next year's target	39%
Two-year target	37%

Knowing these numbers makes clear what the plan is and the timeline for reaching it.)

☐ When there is a gap between what is likely to happen and the target, is there a project that shows how the gap will be closed and on what timeline?

☐ Do department plans reflect the impact of external projects?

☐ Does everyone on the team know their responsibilities for targets and projects? Are their project outcomes clear?

☐ Is there a deadline for breaking down their responsibilities and projects into supporting detail? (This is a cascading process. First, the team gets on the same page about key projects. Then individuals take their assignments and flesh them out in more detail.)

☐ Is there a deadline for sign-off on the plans for the next quarter/next year? (If you are sloppy about plan approval dates, it means your planning is sloppy too.)

Although planning as a team builds team understanding, it is not done in sufficient detail, which leads to the next step—planning one-on-one.

3. Plan One-on-one

The desire to win is in everyone. This is the fundamental premise that comes from the creation narrative. And is a major premise of the leadership model described in this book. Winning means different things to different people, but what's important is that the desire is there.

The desire to win is in everyone.

A primary role of leaders is to get the right people working on the right things. And to get those people fully engaged in using their abilities to contribute to the purposes of the organization and their own need to win.

This requires building strong relationships one-on-one. The following chart shows that the more time you spend with an individual, up to about five hours a week, the more engaged they are. These interactions need not all take place in a formal meeting. All individual interactions, including phone, email, or hallway conversations, count (Figure 10.4).

This principle is modeled repeatedly in the Bible. Jesus narrowed his focus to twelve, and within the twelve, three received more time. He then talked with individuals one-on-one. A more explicit reference to the value of one-on-one interaction (mentioned in Chapter 6) is the analogy of "one person sharpening another," like iron sharpening iron—the imagery of strength against strength.

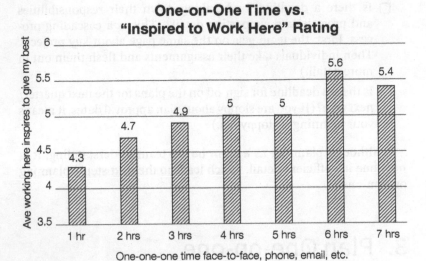

FIGURE 10.4   Inspired to work here.
Source: leadershipiq.com

Not every situation permits one-on-one attention. But the graph tells you that undivided attention is different than group attention in terms of impact.

I notice that in the time I spend with my grandchildren. I have four grandsons under ten in the same family. When I arrange one-on-one time with them, the conversation differs greatly from the chaos of them together. One-on-one conversations are more focused and less influenced by what others around them may think or say. They also sense and value your undivided attention, contributing to their self-worth and identity. Adults are no different—they need meaningful one-on-one interaction.

The first comment of some leaders, when asked about how much time they spend one-on-one with their workers, especially those with thirty direct reports, is, "I don't have time." What they are saying is, "I have time for turnover, retraining, increased error rates, and all the other firefighting activities."

> What they are saying is, "I have time for turnover, retraining, increased error rates, and all the other firefighting activities."

Depending on whose data you use, turnover costs, on average, one hundred hours of lost productivity for the simplest hourly work and up to two thousand hours for skilled positions. We all have to decide where our time is best invested, retaining and engaging people or hiring and onboarding new ones.

After the group review of plans and individual assignments is clear, it is time to meet one-on-one to clarify individual priorities and get team member input on how to best achieve the department goals.

Similar to the team planning session, the purpose of this meeting is threefold:

- Clarify the individual's responsibilities for the next quarter and spot misalignment issues that didn't surface in the group meeting.
- Develop the individual's ability to build their plans. See how they break down their work. Hand off as much responsibility as possible. Look for ways to get team members to take more ownership.
- Build the relationship. Help people connect to purpose and see how they are contributing to something meaningful. Understand what's important to them and align their needs with the organization's strategy.

Keeping the purposes above in mind, check your answers to the following questions.

Plan One-on-one Checklist

☐ Are responsibilities and measures clear? Are people challenged to take ownership of their responsibilities? (As a shorthand, we refer to these as MORs—measured ongoing responsibilities.)

☐ Are those responsibilities reviewed at least quarterly? For routine responsibilities, are there assignments outside the routine that develop them? Training? Improvement projects? Process improvement teams?

☐ Are plans reviewed and approved before the start of the next quarter? Do people see by your commitment their work is important? Do people feel like leaders have time for them?

☐ Does the planning process engage the individual? Are they encouraged to offer ideas and take ownership? Do they feel listened to?

☐ Are difficult topics addressed when setting plans? Are issues identified and follow-up actions agreed to?

☐ Do leaders and employees see the importance of one-on-one interaction and make it work? Or are they just going through the motions?

☐ Do you have people in positions that leverage their strengths? A recent study of professional baseball players shows they have 20/13 vision. Not everyone can hit a 90-mile-an-hour fastball, and not everyone can do their assigned job. ("Can 10,000 hours of practice make you an expert?" BBC News. https://www.bbc.com/news/magazine-26384712.)

The investment in talking with people one-on-one develops them in ways that nothing else can. And the checklist shows it takes time and skill to do it effectively.

The last topic in this chapter will focus on having a business intelligence (BI) strategy.

4. Implement BI Strategy

The surface level value of business intelligence is knowing progress against plan. Also spotting problems early and diagnosing them as well. If that is all BI did, it would be a home run in terms of value.

But fully implemented, *building* a BI strategy provides the vehicle for developing and maintaining alignment in an organization, for building data-driven leaders. Chaos is ever-present for everyone, from the CEO level with unexpected competitive moves or economic changes to the front lines where someone calls in sick or a machine goes down. Good metrics give us a framework for understanding the impact of surprises and deciding what to do about them. It also supports data-driven decision-making.

> BI strategy provides the vehicle for developing and maintaining alignment in an organization, for building data-driven leaders.

There is no way to build a coherent and aligned BI strategy unless you have a clear organization strategy.

The foundation for a BI strategy starts with the strategic difference identified in the visioning process (key market segments, their requirements, and the growth strategy regarding products/services, markets, channels, and geographies). A handful of these metrics with targets should drive the organization's core business model.

There is no way to build a coherent and aligned BI strategy unless you have a clear organization strategy. You can implement BI to support current operations, which will improve some dimension of communication and management focus. But by itself, it will not tighten organizational alignment unless there is something to align with.

Strategy metric definition should lead to the assignment of responsibilities, which then should lead to what supporting activities will drive those results and who is responsible. The metrics must be optimized for different types of work—for example, natural garden (creativity), orchestra (precision), or football (agility).

The metrics also must compensate for the weakness of the organizational structure. For example, functional organization structures optimize for functional expertise but create siloed thinking as opposed to cross-functional client-facing processes.

Larger organizations sometimes organize by markets (geographic) and others by product line. Each has its advantages. BI strategy is structurally agnostic and provides a way to monitor structure weaknesses.

A Few Cautions on BI

People will focus on what you choose to measure, so choose wisely. The power of measures is they define what winning means to people and taps into their built-in desire to do just that. This truth can work for you or against you. For example, in the following exhibit the person managing cash would make very different decisions depending on which of the following measures were used: cash on hand (in dollars) as one measure or sales days of cash as the other (see Figure 10.5).

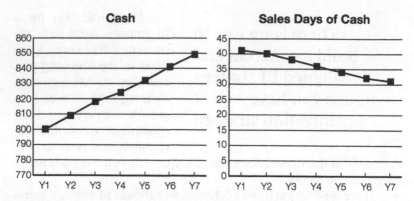

FIGURE 10.5 Sales days of cash.

The power of measures is they define what winning means to people and taps into their built-in desire to do just that. This truth can work for you or against you.

Cash on hand is an *absolute measure* of total cash on hand. Sales days of cash is a *relative measure* and divides total cash by the average daily sales. The absolute approach shows that cash in terms of funds available is growing. It looks good on the graph. But the relative approach shows that cash reserves decline relative to the growing business, which will become a problem in time. Choosing appropriate measures is a learned skill.

Also, having too many measures is distracting. Almost fifty years ago, Theodore Levitt was prophetic when, in his 1974 book *Marketing for Business Growth* (McGraw-Hill, 1974), he explained the challenge we all face: "The more abundant the information, the less meaning it will yield. We know that the surest way to destroy a [person's] capacity for discrimination is to overwhelm his [or her] senses with relevant stimuli."

Read on for business intelligence implementation ideas.

BI Strategy Checklist

☐ Are strategic measures with targets defined? Are they understood throughout the organization?

☐ Does every department and individual have metrics that tie into the strategic measures? Is there an overall architecture to keep metrics lean and focused on vital strategic priorities? Is there a control function responsible for the oversight of the BI strategy?

☐ Are measures easily accessible? Is the definition of metrics standardized so everyone can find what they are looking for? Or do people have to look at several systems?

☐ Are strategic processes measured, allowing for the outcomes to be measured?

☐ Are measures optimized for decision time frames? Can you spot daily hot spots that need attention? How about weekly, monthly, and annual trends? How do these different time horizons affect the visualization design?

☐ Are measures that are not used eliminated? Or does the list of metrics just keep growing in bureaucratic fashion? Is the measuring system lean and mean at the individual level? Does it give each person three to four things to focus on, maximum?

With the completion of planning and business intelligence, we are ready to move on to the next chapter about getting results.

The more abundant the information, the less meaning it will yield. We know that the surest way to destroy a [person's] capacity for discrimination is to overwhelm his [or her] senses with relevant stimuli.

Takeaways

• Operational planning is the collision of two priority worlds—short-term operating needs and long-term strategic change.

• To plan operations properly, external project requirements affecting the team need to be identified and planned so local department implications are understood.

- Leaders should be clear about *what* needs to be accomplished over the next couple of years in terms of targets, but ideally the *how* can be a group dialogue.

- Planning as a group is an investment in building understanding that makes the team more agile as it responds to changes. The understanding is more important than the actual plans because the plans change.

- Alignment cannot be fully achieved in the group setting, and careful investment in one-on-one conversations is necessary to build relationships and alignment and develop team members. It is an illusion when leaders think they don't have time to do this because it costs them more in the end if they don't in terms of turnover, errors, and productivity.

- Business intelligence is foundational for two reasons. First, so that you can track progress and identify issues early. Second, and even more important, the process of defining metrics facilitates a level of alignment not achievable any other way.

CHAPTER 11

Get Results through Teamwork

Know well the condition of your flocks,
and give attention to your herds,
for riches do not last forever....

Proverbs 27

I n the previous chapter the focus was on building clear priorities and getting agreement from the team on how to move forward. This chapter will focus on working that plan and getting the right things done—executing against goals.

Former Notre Dame coach Lou Holtz supposedly said that "when everything is said and done, more gets said than done."

We have to face the reality that the tactics for reaching our goals are always changing.

Everything we have discussed so far doesn't matter unless leaders get results. Or, as Jesus said, "You will know them by their fruit," speaking about the reality of results.

In this chapter, we will have to face the reality that the tactics for reaching our goals are always changing. That becomes clear about fifteen minutes into the day. The question all leaders face is how to get the right things done *today*, balancing the urgent and the important.

The following four best practices will help. Before moving ahead, remember that sequence matters. In this step, the prior work of setting vision, changing strategy, and selecting near-term operating priorities is what sets up success at this stage.

> ## Setting vision, changing strategy, and selecting near-term operating priorities is what sets up success at this stage.

Building on the importance of sequence, another leadership principle related to sequence hides in plain sight in the creation story. Bringing order requires establishing some rhythms. In the creation narrative, the creation of the sun and the moon serve as "signs for seasons, and for days and years" (Genesis 1). We hardly notice, but our lives are organized around a few basic cycles—a twenty-four-hour day, a seven-day week, twelve months, and four seasons.

These cycles are accepted by society and organize how we work, sleep, rest, and just plain live. They bring order that we depend on. How could we communicate our plans or coordinate actions if it weren't for a calendar?

We advocate leaders to establish the following four habits with their teams to execute plans and develop their team.

1. Know and report progress;
2. Synch one-on-one;
3. Synch with team;
4. Step Back and Learn.

In Chapter 13, under "'Own' Team Development" you will be encouraged to build a plan that fits your team's needs regarding the four habits above. That plan becomes your strategy for building and managing your team.

1. Know and Report Progress

What does it mean to lead yourself?

In Chapter 6, we discussed some traits of a self-leader such as openness and honesty and being action oriented. But the bottom line of what it means to be a self-leader is:

- Know what you are responsible for;
- Own the delivery of it;
- Know whether you are on track to deliver;
- Keep people informed of your progress.

A team is only as strong as the self-leadership of its individuals.

As a team leader, clear expectations need to be set as to the standard used for self-reporting: what needs to be reported and how often. The basis of this should come from the one-on-one planning (see Chapter 10). Every person should have a one-page description of their measured ongoing responsibilities (MORs).

> The key to making this habit work is that the policies you set fit the needs of the team *and* they are practiced consistently.

Some people have repetitive work that doesn't need as much coordination. Others do a lot of project work where much coordination is needed. Some employees are less experienced and need more detailed reporting for a period. Leaders need to set some standard for exception reporting, where certain types of things are reported immediately.

The key to making this habit work is that the policies you set fit the needs of the team *and* they are practiced consistently. They become habits that everyone on the team can depend on for mutual benefit.

Know and Report Progress Checklist

☐ Do you understand it is your job to keep your leader informed? Your leader should not have to ask you; report proactively anything they need to know.

☐ Do you have a clear statement of what you are responsible for and how it is measured? Are the targets clear?

☐ Do you have a way (access to data) that tells you your progress toward your goals?

☐ Have you agreed with your leader on the frequency and approach for reporting your progress? Are you following it? Does it make sense to you?

☐ If you are a production worker working at a machine or in a highly repetitive situation, can you step back and report on how the overall process you are part of is working? What could be improved?

☐ When you report progress is there a clear way to show whether you are concerned about meeting your target and why?

☐ Are you growing in your ability to understand why you are off plan? External process barriers, or other constraints? Are you able to contribute thoughtful insight about how to address issues?

☐ Does your team appreciate knowing if you are off track and support you in getting back on track? Do you feel free to be honest about your progress?

☐ Do you have an open relation with your leader and can be candid and will be heard?

☐ Do you feel you "own" your job? Do you take pride in your work and your contribution? Are you growing in your sense of ownership, moving beyond minimum requirements?

The quality of self-reporting sets up the next habit—synch one-on-one.

2. Synch One-on-one

Recall the quote at the beginning of this chapter: "Know well the condition of your flocks, and give attention to your herds." The root of leadership is building relationships around shared purpose. Relationships are the bonding force that holds the "atoms" together.

The purpose of this habit is to:

• Understand how the employee is doing as an individual. Has anything changed at work or at home that is affecting their mindset?

- Review their progress. Coach them to identify gaps and what to do about it. Identify barriers you as a leader need to address.
- Understand their progress against goals and identify any barriers that they need help with.
- Make adjustment in priorities based on the latest information.
- Identify anything that affects the team that needs to be added to the team synch agenda.
- Verify alignment of what they are going to focus on between now and your next meeting.

> The root of leadership is building relationships around shared purpose. Relationships are the bonding force that holds the "atoms" together.

Overall, as a leader, you are attempting to identify issues early. It could be issues with the individual themselves, such as dissatisfaction or problems with someone else, issues that put team goals at risk, or opportunities for long-term development.

Doing this well requires consideration of the type of work and the interdependencies. Following are some questions to think through.

Synch One-on-one Checklist

☐ How dependent is the team on this person's work? High interdependency may require more frequent one-on-ones.

☐ How predictable is the work they do? Is it highly repetitive and the output varies little? That may suggest less frequent meetings. Or are there frequent surprises to be addressed?

☐ How experienced is the person in their work? Do they need more or less oversight?

☐ How long has the individual been with the team? Until they understand the culture and are bonded as part of the team meet more often.

☐ Regardless of the "business" need for frequency, how often do you need to meet to maintain a good relationship?

☐ Do you understand the person's communication style and personality? Consider using personality assessments to understand them and help them understand you. (See Chapter 15.)

☐ Are there recurring issues that are not getting addressed? Don't allow issues to get swept under the rug and ignored. Identify and address questions and concerns from you or the other person promptly.

☐ Do you track follow-up actions so you can hold yourself or the individual for the next meeting? You want to take your follow-up actions seriously if you expect them to.

☐ Are you setting the bar of excellence you want in these meetings? Do you challenge and encourage people to take ownership? Do you expect enough or too much from them?

This one-on-one synch habit interrelates with the team synch meeting, which we cover next. Doing one-on-one synch well allows team meetings to focus on team issues and not waste time on individual issues. That is the next topic.

3. Synch as a Team

For some, meetings have become a four-letter word. But meetings are not the problem; it's the way we use them.

If you type *meeting effectiveness* into a search engine, you'll get a flood of headlines about how much time we waste in meetings. What's wrong with them? How to fix them? Meetings, it seems, have become synonymous with dysfunction and inefficiency.

The starting place for more effective meetings is to change our thinking. If humans were organic cells in a body with no innovative capability, just cogs in a machine, we wouldn't need meetings. Collaborating in a shared conversation is a uniquely human capability. As one meeting attendee noted in a *Harvard Business Review* article titled "Stop the Meeting Madness":

> If humans were organic cells in a body with no innovative capability, just cogs in a machine, we wouldn't need meetings.

I believe that our abundance of meetings at our company is the Cultural Tax we pay for the inclusive learning environment that we want to foster...and I'm ok with that. If the alternative to more meetings is more autocratic decision-making, less input from all levels throughout the organization, and fewer opportunities to ensure alignment and communication by personal interaction, then give me more meetings any time!
"Stop the Meeting Madness" (Harvard Business Review. https://hbr.org/2017/07/stop-the-meeting-madness)

So I start from the position that collaboration is a must. The question is how to do it well. There is no shortage of articles on how to make meetings effective. Although there are useful techniques involving the basics of meeting management, not one of those articles I have read identifies the first requirement for good meetings.

> The team leader must take responsibility for its effectiveness. The goal of every meeting must be effectiveness.

Here it is: the team leader must take responsibility for its effectiveness. The goal of every meeting must be effectiveness. But what does *effective* mean? Like any other goal, you must decide how to measure effectiveness, assign responsibility, and track results. If you lead a group, you *must* own whether the meetings add value. It is your job to determine effectiveness for your team and ensure it is happening. The alternative is waste, disengagement, and poor team performance.

Many managers complain about how much time they spend in meetings. Yet a leader's job is to allocate and develop the resources that align with the organization's vision. It requires constant attention. How are you going to do that without meetings?

It is your job to spend time with people one-on-one and in group settings to guide, coach, and encourage them. A full-time manager's job is not to write code, build spreadsheets, write marketing copy, or do the other things your team is supposed to do.

Your job is to equip them to do their job, run interference, and remove roadblocks—and yes, that requires more meetings. Leaders should make their meetings purposeful and expect the meetings they attend to be purposeful.

> A full-time manager's job *is not to write code, build spreadsheets, write marketing copy, or do the other things your team is supposed to do.*

Running effective meetings is a skill. It takes time, attention, training, and measurement to get it right and to keep it right. You can't set it and forget it.

Following is a checklist to guide your thinking. Admittedly, this list is a tall order. For meaningful collaboration, the team must step up its game and the leader must take ownership that it does.

Synch as a Team Checklist

☐ Do you have a strategy for your meetings? How often and when will you update plans? How often and when will you check in to resolve short-term issues? How often will you review bigger-picture results?

☐ Do you have a data strategy for your meetings? Does the BI approach defined in Chapter 10 provide the information you need for each of your meetings? The data you need for a daily stand-up meeting differs from a weekly meeting and that differs from a monthly review.

☐ Have you asked your team what makes meetings useful to them? What type of information do they need? How often? In what format? Do you verify they get what they need? Will they tell you honestly if meetings are not working? If not, what is wrong with your relationship? How do you fix it?

☐ Are there clear expectations for meeting preparation? Are written status updates sent before the meeting? Is there a deadline for sending them so people can read them? Is the agenda published in time to prepare?

☐ Is there a good meeting discipline that fits the purpose of the meeting? For example, is this a brainstorming meeting? A problem identification meeting or a problem-solving meeting? Are time commitments honored? Are assignments and follow-up tracked and meeting notes distributed? Does the agenda hold people accountable for prior assignments? Are decisions made and recorded? Are notes sent out promptly after the meeting?

☐ Is there a culture of openness and participation? Do people express ideas or concerns without personal attacks? Can people disagree constructively, understanding that the overall aim is better results? Do the meetings raise the performance of the group? Promote high standards?

☐ Does the group share responsibility for meeting effectiveness? Has the leader conveyed how important effective meetings are and that it takes a team effort to make them happen?

☐ Are you, as the leader of the meeting, setting the tone of excellence you expect from your team? Does the quality of your meetings and follow-up actions make a positive statement about what you expect?

I used to advocate that leaders delegate the running of meetings to someone on their staff so they could listen. There are benefits to that, but it often becomes an abdication of responsibility. Meetings are one of the most important tools a leader has; no one else is responsible for making them effective.

Just like leaders have to take responsibility for effective meetings, they must ensure open issues or problems get resolved.

4. Step Back and Learn

Strong leaders *build* strong leaders by their purpose, words and most of all by their actions. I repeat the Bible proverb mentioned in Chapter 6, "as iron sharpens iron, so one man (person) sharpens another."

In this habit we step back from the detailed input on a daily/ weekly basis to mentoring for overall development of the individual. Are they growing in their ability to lead themselves or others?

But is that really true? If you did three a week and spent thirty minutes each, it would take you less than 5% of your time.

We recommend this be completed quarterly for every employee. It follows the typical quarterly planning cycle so it is a natural time to see how prior goals were met. It is infrequent enough that you can step back from the urgent issues of the day. However, some people who supervise twenty or thirty people say there is no way to make the time to do this. But is that really true? If you did three a week and spent thirty minutes each, it would take you less than 5% of your time.

> This meeting is not a performance review. It is a mentoring session with two-way dialogue.

I don't have empirical data on this, but I notice a strong correlation between high turnover and the number of people managed by one supervisor. With more interaction between employees and getting to know them, could turnover be improved?

This meeting is not a performance review. It is a mentoring session with two-way dialogue. We recommend an agenda something like:

- Team member evaluates their own achievement of responsibilities.
- The team member identifies barriers to their own success.
- The team leader evaluates how the team member is seeing their own work.
- Lessons learned since the last review session are identified and developmental projects are identified going forward.
- An overall pulse of the relationship is taken to understand any changes in professional or personal issues that affect the future.
- Relationships are strengthened.
- Follow-up actions by both parties are documented and acted on.
- Good notes are maintained to make it easier to incorporate in annual reviews.
- As you think through how to do this, it is helpful to consider the following.

Step Back and Learn Checklist

☐ Check your motive. Do you believe spending quality time to aid their growth will also improve team results?

☐ Do you have the time to do this mentoring right? If not, why not? Discuss with your leader why this is and what to do about it.

☐ Are you a student of the people in your group? Do you pay attention to what excites them and what discourages them? How they like to communicate?

☐ Do you make these mentoring sessions a priority? Do you prepare for them? Do you conduct them on the agreed upon schedule?

☐ Do you identify follow-up actions from the meeting and assure they get addressed? Does your follow-up set the tone of excellence you want from the individual?

☐ Does your approach work for entry-level workers who may never have thought about what it means to be a self-leader? Can you start with the basics such as attendance? Then grow them to thinking about the next step in maturity?

I want to close this chapter with an observation about new challenges facing leaders. Based on the anecdotal feedback I hear from organization leaders, in the US we have an increasing number of people entering the workforce who really have never been "parented." By this, people mean that recruits haven't learned the basics of responsibility—showing up on time, working hard, and respecting themselves or others.

As leaders, we have to remind ourselves that these recruits, no matter what their maturity is today, have potential as humans. But the question is whether you can provide enough structure, feedback, and direction to build them into self-leaders—responsible people. And of course, you need to determine whether they even *want* to grow into that kind of person. Many do not, at least not yet. Be encouraged that as you grapple with these issues you are doing important work, far more than you may realize. Our organizations and society itself depends on building the next generation of self-leaders.

In the next chapter we will explore another way to engage the natural creativity built into every person.

Takeaways

- Plans are never right. Their value is in the understanding built by the group that prepared them and to provide a framework for how you react to them.

- In a world full of chaos, establishing some repeatable habits on a regular schedule gives people a framework for coordinating with each other.

- To get results through teamwork requires each team member to know their responsibilities and to be held accountable for them. Teamwork is destroyed without it.

- Employee engagement and productivity is directly correlated to one-on-one interaction between team member and leader. Leaders must learn to invest quality one-on-one time mentoring team members and helping them succeed.

- We love to slander the idea of meetings, but purposeful meetings are a primary tool for leaders to maintain alignment and engagement.

- There is great value in stepping back from the weekly perspective, which focuses on the urgent, to a quarterly perspective. This allows focus on the bigger-picture learnings of employee development.

CHAPTER 12

Get Everyone Innovating

For he (farmer) is rightly instructed; his God teaches him. Dill is not threshed with a threshing sledge, nor is a cart wheel rolled over cumin, but dill is beaten out with a stick, and cumin with a rod. Does one crush grain for bread? No, he does not thresh it forever; when he drives his cart wheel over it with his horses, he does not crush it

Isaiah 28

Now we will focus on how to tap into the tremendous knowledge of the people not traditionally thought of as leaders—those on the front lines.

There is deep respect in the Bible for the work people do and the wisdom behind it. Work is holy in God's eyes because He commissioned us to have dominion—to bring order out of chaos. That is the essence of what work means.

The creation narrative continues in chapter 2 of Genesis and shows that God gave Adam the assignment to take care of the Garden of Eden. This work was not a punishment; it was a direct assignment from God before any trouble emerged later in the story. Work is good and holy.

A second example is when God tells Moses to assign Bezalel (a craftsman) a role in the construction of their tabernacle. This is what He says:

> *I have filled him with the Spirit of God in wisdom, in understanding, in knowledge, and in all kinds of craftsmanship to make artistic designs for work in gold, in silver and in bronze and the cutoff stones for settings, and in the carving of wood....*
> *Exodus 31*

The most basic premise of the Bible is that *everyone* is created in God's image and has incalculable worth. He longs for us to grow to know Him more as we work and live and battle the surrounding chaos. This is our calling.

Inspiring everyone to innovate is a double win. First, you improve business results. Second, you increase opportunities for individuals to win (to have an idea and create an impact). Since everyone *needs* to win, you can unleash exceptional engagement and satisfaction by helping them see how.

> Too often, people grow up hearing about what they "can't do" and what their limitations are.

Too often, people grow up hearing about what they "can't do" and what their limitations are. It is hard work to build an organization that believes everyone has impressive abilities to contribute beyond their job description. It is swimming against the stream. It is bringing a new level of order to the surrounding chaos.

Bottom-up Focus

Organizations drive change for two different reasons and from two different directions. Strategic change is driven top-down and requires external analysis and a holistic view of the organization and the environment it operates within.

Continuous improvement is driven from the bottom of the organization and is focused primarily on improving the way existing processes work.

Driving change from the bottom-up is implemented differently than from the top-down, and it has its own barriers.

Barriers to Bottom-up Change

In our work, we have seen three barriers to unleashing this latent capability.

- Missing the potential. Leaders sometimes do not understand the potential this opportunity presents. Do the math. In a 500-person organization, about 15% of people (75) will be supervisory. So 425 people with the human capacity to innovate are not part of the management process and much less input to decisions.

- No belief in self. The second barrier is that individuals don't believe in themselves. Many people have had experiences at home, in school, and in other organizations that undermine their belief in their abilities to innovate. They have been told for so long that their job is to do X. And do it in the way they have been trained. If they come up with an idea, some leaders don't know what to do with it, and it dies.

- No system. The third barrier is the lack of a system that assures effective action. This third barrier doesn't matter unless the previous two barriers are overcome.

> Many people have had experiences at home, in school, and in other organizations that undermine their belief in their abilities to innovate.

This is not complicated. But neither is staying fit. You exercise, eat right, and keep doing it. It sounds simple, but it requires dedication and commitment to see results. In this chapter, we'll look at two ideas that work if leaders commit to them.

The first is a traditional suggestion system for anyone to provide input on any topic. The second approach is for self-managing teams to manage processes proactively.

1. Act on Ideas

Many organizations have tried suggestion box approaches. They seldom gain long-term traction. People believe nothing will happen, and eventually, they stop contributing ideas. To change that culture

To change that culture of disbelief and disengagement, you need to use the kindling approach for starting a fire.

of disbelief and disengagement, you need to use the kindling approach for starting a fire. Begin with a small spark, and nurture it.

The critical factor is to create an idea system where ideas are acted on promptly. Posters, slogans, and company meetings are all talk; it is the *implementation* of ideas that creates excitement. Remember, people want to win. Seeing one of your ideas implemented and working is a win. It is not just a means to better organizational performance; it is also an end that is satisfying to the employee.

The key elements for an engaging system are:

- Self-managing teams have the authority to evaluate and implement ideas. No red tape, clear funding sources.
- A strong champion(s) from the front lines who is well supported by an executive sponsor.
- A simple process for gathering and evaluating ideas.
- A process for implementing ideas and tracking results so they can be reported.

What doesn't work is a suggestion box that turns into a black hole where ideas disappear. The box becomes a system for filing complaints and delegating problems to the management team.

A few questions for you to consider.

Act on Ideas Checklist

☐ Is senior management behind this, or is it a fad item on the checklist?

☐ Is there a training program that helps team managers make this work? Just like senior leadership has to believe, so do front-line managers. They won't all come onboard at once, but there has to be a couple who show everyone else the way.

☐ Is there a non-management champion somewhere that helps start the process?

☐ Is there a simple technology for quickly capturing ideas? Production floor kiosks? Smartphones? Break room?

☐ Is there a self-managing team where ideas get evaluated? Does this process differentiate between easy-to-implement actions and those that need formal project management? Is there organizational support in terms of executive sponsorship, budget, etc.?

☐ Are people on the front lines involved in implementation? They understand why the change is being made and can evaluate whether it works better than anyone else. Also, involving them fulfills their desire to win.

☐ Is the impact of ideas measured? Is that impact visible and celebrated in team meetings and other corporate communication?

☐ Does the process work? If not, is someone determined to diagnose what's wrong and get it working? Are valuable ideas being implemented? Do you have the leadership in place to make this work? (If you don't, stop it.)

Let's move on to process management. This approach is independent of the "Act on Ideas" approach and should therefore be implemented separately.

2. Manage Processes Proactively

If your business isn't running right, you likely have a process problem.

Either you have a missing process, a poorly defined process, or you're not properly managing the processes you have. Many businesses haven't identified their core processes, so they can't tell if they're working based on measurable data. Yet businesses rise or fall based on the effectiveness of those same processes.

> At the root of the value of process management is organized learning. To improve something you must learn, and to learn you must measure.

A process is an ordered set of activities that produces a planned result. Qualifying a sales lead is an example of a process. A recipe for baking bread is a process. Processes are like blueprints that describe how the business works and how it keeps its promises to stakeholders.

At the root of the value of process management is organized learning. To improve something you must learn, and to learn you must measure (observe results). James Harrington captures the significance of this learning cycle in this quote:

"Measurement is the first step that leads to control and eventually to improvement. If you can't measure something, you can't understand it. If you can't understand it, you can't control it. If you can't control it, you can't improve it" (H. James Harrington, "(25 Inspirational Business Process Improvement Quotes: from teamguru.com)."

Conceptually it is straightforward, but learning to manage processes systematically takes time and skill development. The difficulty of managing processes compounds because every aspect related to the process is constantly changing. The customer changes, our services change, the people executing the processes change, and the organizational strategy changes. It is just another form of chaos that has to be continuously managed or it compounds to being out of control.

> Organizations that have not been managing processes may feel overwhelmed about where to start. That feeling itself can become the enemy.

Organizations that have not been managing processes may feel overwhelmed about where to start. That feeling itself can become the enemy and freeze organizations from action. So what do you do? Israel faced a similar situation thousands of years ago coming out of 400 years of slavery and needing to form a nation from scratch. They had no processes or systems or even any land on which to live. The quote below shows the direction God gave them.

Remember not the former things, nor consider the things of old. Behold, I am doing a new thing; now it springs forth, do you not perceive it? I will make a way in the wilderness and rivers in the desert.

Isaiah 43:20

> The principle is the same. Don't dwell on the past. Focus on the future, and get busy "making your way."

The context is much bigger. God is talking about saving a whole nation from their own folly, but the principle is the same. Don't dwell on the past. Focus on the future, and get busy "making your way" on the challenges in front of you.

We don't have God's power or wisdom in the business world, so we narrow our focus to something we can manage. We pick one process, define what it should do, and unleash the right people to improve it. Compared to idea generation, process management offers the benefit of a team relationship, shared purpose, and the opportunity to involve many people across different processes. It is an organized way to leverage the untapped potential of many front-line people in the organization.

The following is a checklist of questions to consider as you design your process management approach.

Manage Processes Proactively Checklist

☐ Do you have a list of the major processes that drive your success? At the strategy level for the entire organization? Within your department?

☐ Do you have a classification system for managing processes? Following is an example:

- **Simple:** Not documented. Typically one person handles it, not changing much;
- **Unmanaged:** Not documented, multiple people involved, cross-functional, unpredictable;
- **Managed:** Team responsible, documented, designed, measured, cross-functional, improving;
- **Mature:** Managed and has operated predictably for three years.

☐ Are unmanaged processes prioritized?

☐ Is a process management team formed to manage this process? Does the team have the right mix of people on it? Do people have the time to contribute to this process?

☐ Has the process team documented how the process works? Is the team trained on process documentation and management? What policies affect the process implementation? Are policy issues elevated to the right people? Do those people support the resolution of those issues?

☐ Is the current process performance known? Does the team understand the gap between the vision target and the actual results that are occurring?

☐ Is the measure and vision target set for the process selected? Do this process and its outcome tie into the organization's key measures?

☐ Does the team thoroughly analyze a recommended change before adoption? Are implementation risks managed?

☐ Is the team in a regular rhythm of small, targeted improvements? Do they set an improvement target? Is change controlled so that the team understands what caused improvement?

☐ Does the rest of the organization understand who handles the process? Does the "idea" system in the previous section tie into the process teams so that appropriate ideas flow to them?

☐ Are process outcomes predictable? Can you trust the process works reliably? Is the overall management process working?

Managing critical processes provides an effective way to manage cross-functional coordination in fast-growing organizations and engages more people in contributing to the continuous innovation that drives higher quality and better results. The net effect is a culture where chaos no longer reigns. Issues get identified and addressed, and people feel empowered to make their work lives better and more satisfying. And the organization grows without outgrowing its own ability to execute.

The next chapter will describe how leaders can step back from the details of everyday operation and develop strategies for preparing their teams for the future.

Takeaways

- About 85% of workers are not in the loop in the normal planning process. They have lots of ideas and ability to contribute.

- One way to enhance participation is a system to capture ideas and have a process for seeing that they get acted on promptly.

- Getting traction is a cultural change that requires grass roots, front-line leadership, and quick wins to overcome jaded attitudes from past experiences with suggestion boxes.

- Another model is proactive process management where key processes have standing teams assigned to design and improve processes.

- The key to managing processes is clear metrics that prove the process is dependable and improving.

CHAPTER 13

Prepare
Their Team
for the Future

*...this year you shall eat what grows of itself,
and in the second year what springs from that?
Then in the third year sow and reap,
and plant vineyards, and eat their fruit.*

Isaiah 37

Growing up in an agricultural community you learn to think ahead. Taking shortcuts in soil preparation, seed quality, or weed control affects the crop in the fall. Taking shortcuts in fertilization, crop rotation, and drainage affects yields for years to come.

This chapter will challenge leaders to step back, think, and act on what it takes to prepare their teams for the future.

You Get What You Repeat

In *Atomic Habits*, James Clear reminds us that *repeatable* habits are the key to getting what you want tomorrow.

> Your weight is a lagging measure of your eating habits. Your knowledge is a lagging measure of your learning habits. Your clutter is a lagging measure of your cleaning habits. You get what you repeat.

Your outcomes are a lagging measure of your habits. *Your net worth is a lagging measure of your financial habits. Your weight is a lagging measure of your eating habits. Your knowledge is a lagging measure of your learning habits. Your clutter is a lagging measure of your cleaning habits. You get what you repeat.*

James Clear. Atomic Habits *(p. 18). Penguin Publishing Group. Kindle Edition.*

When you apply this principle to leadership, your team's success will be a function of the habits you and your team develop. This is one way you prepare your team for the future. You invest in building better habits.

Building into the lives of self and others is a leadership mindset, a "yeast" that spreads into every other best practice discussed in this book.

We start with the habit of "facing the facts."

1. Face the Facts

...and you will know the truth, and the truth will set you free.
Jesus (John 8:31)

The human architecture we discussed in Chapter 4 proposes that desire and thought interact to produce action. Our actions flow out of what we want and what we believe. When Jesus taught his disciples, He required they know the truth about who He was. And that truth, when embraced, brings action that is different and free from the past. For example, if we start to see ourselves differently in terms of our worth, our confidence changes and people see us and treat us differently. We become free of behaviors that were linked to past thinking.

> Since our actions flow out of our beliefs, we have a lot at stake in knowing what is true.

Since our actions flow out of our beliefs, we have a lot at stake in knowing what is true. The linkage is so tight that when we believe wrong things, the Bible refers to it as bondage. The imagery is strong.

Organizations are subject to the same principle. If you don't know the truth about what your customers want or what they think about your products, you are acting out of some other set of beliefs that will probably lead to wrong actions. Leaders of self and others know that the truth is the only path to good long-term outcomes.

Jim Collins references this idea in his book *Good to Great*.

All good-to-great companies began finding a path to greatness by confronting the brutal facts of their current reality.

When you start with an honest and diligent effort to determine the truth of your situation, the right decisions often become self-evident. It is impossible to make moral decisions without infusing the entire process with an honest confrontation of the brutal facts.

A primary task in taking a company from good to great is to create a culture wherein people have a tremendous opportunity to be heard and for the truth to be heard.

Collins, Jim. Good to Great: Why Some Companies Make the Leap.... And Others Don't. *Kindle Edition*

Following are some self-examination questions.

Face the Facts Checklist

☐ Have you created an environment where people openly discuss the facts? Are people more afraid of you than the facts? Do you want to know the truth?

☐ Do you have an approach to assess what is happening outside your team? Outside your company? Technological trends? Economic? Regulatory? Competitive?

☐ Do you have an approach for gathering feedback about what is happening inside your team? Your organization? Does this approach include one-on-one interaction that allows privacy? How about group feedback where synergy can occur?

☐ Does your group embrace this process for improving as a team? Do they see this as a team responsibility, not just a team leader responsibility? Do they believe everyone has unique insights and can contribute?

☐ Do you have some way to gather feedback about the effectiveness of your leadership system and the way you work "on" the business?

☐ Is feedback prioritized and acted on, such as SWOT (strengths, weaknesses, opportunities, threats)?

> Are people more afraid of you than the facts? Do you want to know the truth?

After facing the facts, the next step involves taking ownership of your team's development.

2. "Own" Team Development

Is the development of your team a priority for you? Do you own this responsibility?

You act on what you believe, so the journey starts with what you believe. Your leadership has to confront what you believe as a leader

> You act on what you believe, so the journey starts with what you believe.

and provide leaders practical tools for developing their teams. This means a *deliberate* approach for the team as a unit *and* the individuals.

The question is how. Following is some background information for your consideration as you think your approach.

- Consider deploying a learn-by-doing approach. Just-in-time learning with real-world problems to solve is more effective than long classroom-type studies jammed with unapplied principles.

- Recognize developing people is important but it falls in not urgent category and therefore is at risk of not getting done. Your team development approach has to provide accountability to make it urgent.

- Think about the cost-benefit trade-off. Developing people is a significant effort. How important is this responsibility? Do I have to do it myself? Mike Rother, the author of the *Toyota Kata Practice Guide*, asked these same questions. Mike studied how Toyota integrated the Kata process into its company culture for years. He says:

> ...managers are by default the teachers—the coaches in our case—because what they say and do every day, deliberately or not, trains and shapes their people's thinking....

...managers are by default the teachers—the coaches in our case—because what they say and do every day, deliberately or not, trains and shapes their people's thinking....

This coaching is done as part of normal daily work, so the coach is probably going to be the learner's supervisor or manager. So, coaching...is, in fact, a way of managing. Mentoring takes time. If you can't invest significant one-on-one time with each of those who report to you, you will have limited success.

For emphasis, I repeat the research from LeadershipIQ I mentioned in Chapter 10 (Figure 13.1). It shows that *employee engagement, productivity, and innovation* continue to increase by up to five hours of one-on-one time per week.

- Tailor your approach to the individual. In Chapter 7, we discussed different leadership models—natural, garden, orchestra, and football. The following checklist illustrates how these different models apply to individuals.

Own Team Development Checklist:

☐ Do you take advantage of tools that help you understand individual personality, such as DISC? Do these help you match people to responsibilities, or improve your ability to communicate?

☐ Do you have a plan for the frequency with which you need to meet each of your employees that fits their specific needs? How detailed do their plans need to be? Is their work highly

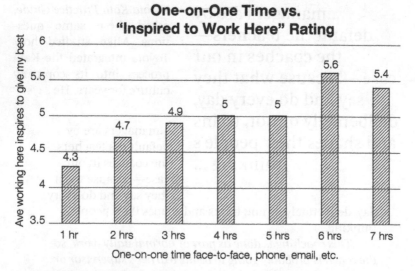

FIGURE 13.1 Increasing employee engagement, productivity, and innovation with one-on-one time.

Source: leadershipiq.com

interdependent? Are they experienced enough to take broad responsibility? Is their work highly recurring and stable? Do they have lots of project work?

☐ Does their plan have specific training objectives with due dates?

☐ Do you have a schedule for meeting with your team? Is there a clear agenda? What metrics will you review on what frequency? Weekly? Monthly? Quarterly? Do you have a subset of employees that are on your executive team? Do you need daily operational huddles? Who attends which meetings?

☐ Do you have a schedule for updating quarterly plans? Group review of plans? Individual review and approval?

☐ Are your meetings predictable? Have they become habits that your team can depend on?

☐ Are you developing candidates to replace you?

☐ Do you have a plan for team development group training separate from individual development?

☐ Is there accountability for the commitments you have made above? Does the system track and report that these important things are getting done? Does your leader hold you accountable?

A consistent development plan supports the final leadership best practice, which is related to delivering quality career-level feedback (often annually).

3. Give Career Feedback

...a good word makes the heart glad.
Proverbs

A "good" word does not mean a "happy" word. "Good" means purposeful, useful, and truthful.

This quote conveys the main idea of this section. Effective leaders give a "good" word to the people they mentor. A "good" word does not mean a "happy" word. "Good" means purposeful, useful, and truthful. It would not be a "good'" word to tell someone they were doing well at work when they weren't. And it is not a "good" word to *withhold* acknowledgment of good work.

A good word is a combination of truth delivered with the right motive—to help someone else fulfill their purpose. When it came to fulfilling this responsibility, for many years I worried about the annual appraisal process. I seldom had the confidence that I was fulfilling my responsibility for giving useful feedback to those who reported to me. Part of this was because I rarely took the time to set meaningful goals or track results.

I also knew that no matter how good my records were, there were other aspects of a person's performance I didn't understand, other people's perspectives. Bottom line, I didn't have the time or information to prepare the way I should, and I would scurry around looking for emails and other documents to have some basis for my input.

> People on the other side of the table have the same discomfort. All too often, both parties seem to have a mutual, unspoken agreement—let's get this over with, so HR gets off our back.

People on the other side of the table have the same discomfort. All too often, both parties seem to have a mutual, unspoken agreement—let's get this over with, so HR gets off our back. It doesn't seem like something so important should feel this way.

Believing that God created everyone in His image, I didn't feel I had much integrity in my approach. Not just as a manager but as a human being. There aren't very many people who can have more impact in someone's life than their employer. Most leaders I know would like to do this better.

Helping address this need (and desire) becomes a requirement for your leadership system. Improving this process depends on many other aspects of leadership that you undertake throughout the year. If you establish those habits, the information-gathering prep work is already complete. This allows you to focus on the qualitative analysis and interpretation you want to provide when you look at the year in retrospect. So what are these habits?

The following checklist revisits many of the other items discussed in earlier chapters that take place during the year.

Give Career Feedback Checklist

☐ Does each employee have a one-page plan that documents ongoing responsibilities and measurements? Is this plan accurate? Does it have the right amount of detail?

☐ Is there a process for gathering progress feedback during the year? Does this encourage employee reflection on their work and quality dialogue with their leader while the results are fresh?

☐ Is there a policy about the use of multi-rater feedback? Is it used effectively? Are people providing constructive input?

☐ Can leaders easily access relevant preparation information, such as last year's review, quarterly feedback, DISC assessments, and multi-rater feedback (if available)?

☐ Has the "during the year" feedback allowed the focus to be forward-looking instead of backward-looking?

☐ Are professional development priorities captured that reflect joint employee and employer interests? Are there timelines and a basis for accountability?

☐ Are review logistics well defined? Are rating policies clear? Is the schedule clear? Is training available and completed on time?

☐ Is the overall process effective? Does the leader provide meaningful input to individual team members? Do team members understand the input and gain value that helps them in their careers?

This is the last step in the leadership system best practices described in the seven chapters of Part 2. At this point, you need a system to clarify what leaders need to do to be effective and to turn those activities into sustainable habits.

Now we will transition to Part 3, which moves from building managerial process skills to people engagement skills.

Takeaways

- An important leadership responsibility that often gets pushed aside by the chaos is preparation of the team for the future. Similarly, the Bible coaches parents to "train up a child in the way he should go; even when he is old he will not depart from it" (Proverbs 22).

- This preparation requires the ability to gather and face the facts about what is happening outside the group you don't control and what is happening inside the group that you do.

- Leaders should create a plan for every single person on the team and for the team as a group. This plan should include training and the time and frequency of one-on-one and team meetings.

- Because of it is likely this responsibility gets pushed off, there should be some sort of tracking or accountability process to make this important responsibility more urgent.

- Leaders should be a student of each of their employees through clear responsibility definition and one-on-one mentoring so that at least once a year they can step back and provide bigger-picture guidance to the team member on their strengths and weaknesses and fit to the individual career desires.

PART 3

What Effective Leaders Should Be

"Being" is a higher standard than "doing." I can paint pictures (doing) and not *be* an artist. So it is with leadership. We can give you the system and checklists as in Part 2 and you can do those things and still not *be* a leader.

In Part 3 we will shift from the process aspects of leadership to the people dimension. It is in this section that we grapple with the challenge of how to bring life to the processes (Part 2) by engaging people at the heart and mind level.

> Yes, we need process and technology to attain new heights, but the upside *and* downside of sustainable human progress is most often based on our attitudes and interpersonal behavior.

When you couple people skills with process skills you can avoid the bureaucracy that systems can bring. See the upper left quadrant of the following image. We know from Part 1 of the book that humans are creatures of desire. Our actions flow from our desires.

Sustainable Leadership Effectiveness

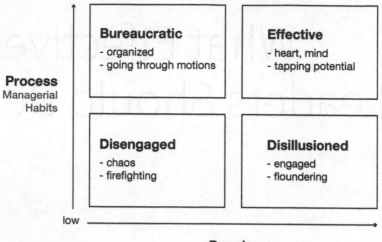

Source: LeadFirst.ai

Therefore, the processes we reviewed in Part 2 of the book are only useful if they help people achieve their purposes and fulfill desires.

In the following chapters we will describe a model of the people skills that are necessary to sustain success. Ongoing effectiveness requires that those who are leading other people must exemplify these behaviors and must foster their development in the people they lead.

Yes, we need process and technology to attain new heights, but the upside *and* downside of sustainable human progress is most often based on our attitudes and interpersonal behavior. I wish I could look you in the eye and repeat what I just said. Please reread the previous sentence. It is there where we most frequently fall short.

This last part of the book is the capstone of our journey together. Let's move forward into the next chapter and dig into the most foundation leadership behavior.

Part 3 chapters are:

14. Someone Who Cares for People
15. Honest and Open
16. Someone Who Builds Oneness
17. Takes Ownership
18. Someone Who Masters Mentoring

CHAPTER 14

Someone Who Cares

Above all, keep loving one another earnestly, since love covers a multitude of sins.

1 Peter 4

When it comes to building effective organizations, what is the human relationship equivalent of the bonding force that holds atoms together? That is the question every leader must answer. And it is the subject of this chapter.

Whatever that force is, it has to be powerful enough to overcome the unique desires of the people, which tend to push us apart. In my four decades of experience it is by far the greatest leadership challenge of all.

The Bible speaks a great deal about the forces that bind people together. There are four, one of which is especially applicable to us as leaders in a business setting.

Four Types of Relational Bonding

The latter part of the Bible is written in Greek. Four different Greek words are translated or alluded to as *love* in English. These words represent four different types of love:

- **Family love.** The Greek word is *storge*. This is the natural affection that occurs in a healthy family. We are instinctually bonded and have a source of trust and protection. You are born into this kind of relationship.

- **Friendship love.** The Greek word is *phileo*. This represents close relations you choose to develop as opposed to being born into. Healthy friendships are based on mutual and reciprocal behaviors of respect, trust, and shared interests. These relationships can come and go.

- **Romantic, sexual love.** The Greek word is *eros*. This attraction is designed into humans. The creation narrative implies it is present to assure that we multiply and fulfill our mission. It is also the basis of a unique "oneness" that we will discuss later.

- **Unconditional love.** The Greek word for unconditional love is *agape*. Agape love is a conscious choice to relate to someone with their best interests in mind, regardless of their response. It is proactive, not reactive. God's love for us falls into this category.

> Agape love is a conscious choice to relate to someone with their best interests in mind, regardless of their response.

Of these four, one is given special attention in the Bible.

The Paradox Answered

The English version of the Bible contains about 800,000 words, most of them speaking about relationships. However, you don't have to run off and try to read it all overnight because God tells us all 800,000 words can be recapped into twenty-five. Here they are:

Love the Lord your God with all your heart and with all your
soul and with all your mind and love your neighbor as yourself.
Matthew 22

Which of the four types of love is it? You guessed it: it's agape. The unilateral, unconditional kind.

> ## Agape love is God's answer to the creation paradox that tells us we are called to rule over the whole earth, but we have to work with other people to do it.

Agape love is God's answer to the creation paradox that tells us we are called to rule over the whole earth, but we have to work with other people to do it. We have to love each other unconditionally. Note that the word *love* is a verb. It requires intentional action.

When we are in a church service, we might think, "This love stuff is good," but we might also think that it doesn't work in business. That is not what the Bible says. It tells us about the laws of the universe and the laws of human interaction. They apply everywhere and all the time. Take it or leave it. You are free to decide.

> ## The idea of treating you right regardless of how you treat me does not sound fun or even practical.

I, too, had to work myself through the objection above, and even after doing so I have an objection I still struggle with. There is a part of the agape love thing I don't like. I want mutual relationships where you do good stuff for me and I, in return, do good stuff for you. The idea of treating you right regardless of how you treat me does not sound fun or even practical.

It reminds me of a premarriage conference Rhonda and I attended years ago. One speaker said that a marriage is not based on a 50/50 relationship. It is based on a 100/100 relationship where my standard of behavior is to always treat my wife right regardless of how she treats me and vice versa. I was thinking, "Yikes, what did I sign up for?"

After years of imperfect application, Rhonda and I realize that we have a much richer relationship based on this principle. It works. It's abundant and much better than the other 50/50 relationships I have.

> Love is centered in what you believe and not reacting to what others do.

Why does it work better? Because the alternative is to go through life in total reaction mode. I react to you, and you react to me, and pretty soon everything has spiraled out of control. Love is centered in what you believe and not reacting to what others do. Agape love comes from God Himself.

In those days when I am not living up to my "100%" behavior standard with Rhonda, she doesn't react (usually). Her guiding compass is to do what's right, regardless. This gives me time to get back on track without adding to the crisis by responding to her reaction to my bad behavior. That road leads to the destruction of the relationship.

Even though this principle is working at home I still have a problem.

My Two-faced Nature

I still don't like the idea of applying this too broadly at work. I want to treat people based on their behavior. After reflecting on this for years, I realize I am hypocritical on this topic. What I really want is for *others*

> What I really want is for *others* to treat me right, regardless of how I treat them. "Do as I say, not as I do."

to treat me right, regardless of how I treat them. "Do as I say, not as I do."

This is what God is trying to tell us with his twenty-five-word recap of the whole Bible. If you want to experience what you are designed for, this is the only way you get it.

You and I both know that we aren't able to do this. We work at it and do it with some people sometimes, but not consistently and not for long. (This conundrum is the very reason Jesus appeared on the scene. His mission was and is to fix broken relationships between us and God and with each other. It is why His mission is called the "good news" in the Bible.)

Now let's look at what I call the people engagement model. The foundation of this model is based on leaders having the character and behavioral skill to build agape-based relationships.

Five Steps to Engagement

Five behaviors build an engaged team, but they are not for the faint of heart. They don't come naturally. Instead, they require us to change.

The five behaviors are shown in Figure 14.1. We start with caring for people at the top of the model. It is foundational because people have a deep-seated need to be valued, to be treated as worthwhile. Truly caring about the people on your team sets up the second behavior, which is honesty and openness. We will cover that in the next chapter. And all the succeeding behaviors in the chapters after that.

The best way to understand the agape approach to caring is a couple of stories.

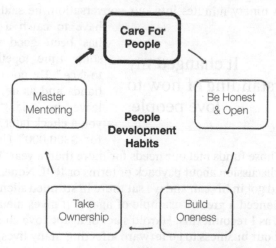

FIGURE 14.1   People engagement model—care for people.

Harold Morgan Flies in from Tulsa

Early in the life of our first business, we ran out of funds. We had exhausted our personal and friends/family resources. As always, Jack, Vern, and I prayed for guidance and kept working. Unexpectedly, Harold Morgan, a friend and business associate of Jack, called Jack just to see how he was doing. Jack reconnected with Harold and shared our progress as a business. Harold was from Tulsa. And he said that he was coming to see us on Monday. He didn't ask; he told us. It was Friday.

We scrambled around thinking that maybe he would invest with us. We prepared presentations about the business and our capital needs. Monday came around, and we met for lunch at a local hotel.

We sat down and ordered our lunch. I got out some presentation materials, and Harold politely said, "Just put that away. I came to see how you are really doing. What is going on in your life? Are you doing okay with your families? With your co-workers? How is life for you?"

We had a lively time of sharing. And Harold always kept the conversation on us. He was there because he was interested in us. There was no other reason. Getting to Findlay, Ohio, is not easy to do. There are no direct flights, and we are two hours from the nearest airport. It easily burns up a half day each way.

About ninety minutes into our conversation, he said, "Well, I have to catch a flight. It has been good to spend some time together face-to-face." He got up, shook hands and as he turned to leave, he said, "I'll send you a check later this week for $300,000" (in today's dollars). Those funds met our needs for more than a year. There was no initial discussion about payback or terms or ROI. None.

> It changed my understanding of how to love people.

Harold got in his car, and we sat there in stunned silence. I have not experienced a greater example of agape. It gives me a lump in the throat as I recount this. Harold's act of agape love changed me. It allowed our business to go forward affecting many lives, but even more, it changed my understanding of how to love people.

Give What's in Your Hand

You may think, great example, but I don't have large funds to give. The beauty of God's standard for loving is that you give from what you have. Not from what someone else has. You always have something to give. Sometimes your best gift is *just* listening and caring. Giving strengthens relationships; unilateral taking destroys them.

> You always have something to give. Sometimes your best gift is *just* listening and caring.

I have another story about giving that cost me nothing. We had a sad case where an employee, David, could not get along with others. He was competent in his work, but unbearable to work with. As CEO, I did not know this individual personally, and he reported to a supervisor two levels below me whom I knew and trusted. It was reported to me by his director that his employment was being terminated. I checked whether we had handled the situation with integrity, and we had.

I felt I should do something for David. I had no motive since he was leaving the company. But there appeared from nowhere within me an agape-like interest in this person. I encourage you to pay attention to these inner leadings in your life.

> I clarified that if he didn't trust me, the conversation was going to be a waste of time.

I emailed David and asked if he would meet with me before he left, and he said yes. I started the meeting by telling him that nothing in this conversation was going to change the decision to terminate him. And then I asked him, "Do you trust me?" I clarified that if he didn't trust me, the conversation was going to be a waste of time. He said he did. I slowly and carefully related the feedback that others had provided me on how he interacted with them, his belligerence, and uncooperativeness and unwillingness to take input. I told him I had no motive other than to help him see himself as others see him.

He broke down in tears. He said he didn't realize he came across that way. And that no one had told him this before. I gently pointed out that was not true. Many people had tried, but he could not "hear" them.

By the end of the conversation, David understood how he came across. I don't know how difficult it was for him to change his behaviors in the future. He sincerely thanked me for helping him. He said it would change his approach in his next job. He seemed relieved and refreshed in his outlook by the end.

> ## Strength of relationships affect our ability to hear truth.

I didn't stay in touch with David, and I don't know what happened. Nevertheless, I tell this story to illustrate a couple of truths. First, strength of relationships affect our ability to hear truth. The relationship between David and his supervisors didn't allow for full communication. My communication got through, I believe, because it was an selfless interaction. I had nothing to gain by meeting with him. He knew with certainty that my motive was concern for him. I suspect that knowledge changed his ability to grasp what I was saying.

We could write a whole book on the topic of caring about people. Instead, I will distill my suggestions into a few tips.

Getting Real—Eight Tips for Caring

- ☐ Do a gut check about your attitude toward other people. Do you care for people as a means to your ends, as a manipulation technique, or as something worthwhile in itself?
- ☐ Spend one-on-one time with your people. Nothing communicates interest more than the time you spend with them.
- ☐ Stay up to date of their life *outside* of work—their family, interests, concerns, and joys.
- ☐ Apologize when you screw up. Do it quickly and mean it. The best way to establish a high standard of behavior is to declare the standard and admit when you don't meet it. No one is perfect. Don't pretend you are.
- ☐ Apply the agape principle of treating people right even if they don't reciprocate. It takes time for people to believe you really

are interested in them. Many will be skeptical because of past experiences.

☐ Don't be a doormat. An agape approach toward relationships can lead to tough love interactions—a combination of truth delivered with a love motive.

☐ Lead by example. Share some of your own interests. Let them see who you are. You can do this without getting into inappropriate personal information.

☐ Learn to ask honest questions that show interest. Questions are powerful because they penetrate more deeply than statements since the brain has to do enough processing to provide an answer.

Our instincts tell us that it is important to care about other people. What we don't realize is that behavior enables people to process truth openly. Failure to do so shuts down communication. This leads us into the next chapter about honesty and openness, but first some additional biblical insights about caring.

> Do you care for people as a means to your ends, as a manipulation technique, or as something worthwhile in itself?

Additional Thoughts about Living Wisely

- "Let each of you look not only to his own interests, but also to the interests of others" (Philippians 2:4).

- "Be kind to one another, tenderhearted, forgiving one another, as God in Christ forgave you" (Ephesians 4:32).

- "But if anyone has the world's goods and sees his brother in need, yet closes his heart against him, how does God's love abide in him? Little children, let us not love in word or talk but indeed and in truth" (1 John 3:17).

- "And let us not grow weary of doing good, for in due season we will reap, if we do not give up. So then, as we have opportunity, let us do good to everyone" (Galatians 6:9–10).

- "Therefore encourage one another and build one another up, just as you are doing" (1 Thessalonians 5:11).

- "Bear one another's burdens, and so fulfill the law of Christ" (Galatians 6:2).

- "Whoever is generous to the poor lends to the LORD, and he will repay him for his deed" (Proverbs 19:17).

- "Put on then, as God's chosen ones, holy and beloved, compassionate hearts, kindness, humility, meekness, and patience" (Colossians 3:12).

CHAPTER 15

Honest and Open

Have I then become your enemy by telling you the truth?

Galatians 4

Love, the topic of the last chapter, is certainly a deep topic, but now we will engage with another challenging but related concept—honesty and openness. We use these terms a lot, but what do they really mean in practice? Why is it the truth can make us angry? Note the quote above from the Apostle Paul to one church he was mentoring. He was trying to help them and yet was perceived as an enemy.

In this chapter, we will explore how openness and honesty affect team bonding. It is the second behavior in the people engagement model, and it depends on the foundation laid in the first step—caring for people.

Trust

Being honest and open is a set of behaviors that allows us to trust each other. It involves knowing what is true, speaking what is true, and not withholding information. It even has an aspect of competency—the ability to deliver what we promise.

FIGURE 15.1 People engagement model—honest and open.

Regardless of motive, we cannot work together and get the benefits of a team if we cannot communicate openly and accurately. This process is undermined by deception, ignorance, or even fear—fear of sharing what we think. Let's illustrate with a true story.

A Father-in-law's Fears

Following is one of my own experiences as a leader where the fear in an employee was stronger than the trust we had built together.

I once had an excellent engineer, Tom, who I thought was fully engaged. Because of budget, we ask a second engineer, Susan, to find other work while she continued to work for us. Susan was another excellent employee but was less experienced and had less tenure with us. We did not want to lose her. It was a tough decision, but financial constraints were real. To assist, we put Susan in contact with another company, and she got an offer and accepted it while she was still working with us.

However, right after Susan accepted the position, Tom gave me two weeks' notice that he was leaving. I asked him why he had not kept me informed about his decision to seek other employment, as we had agreed to when he was hired. He said he had gotten deep into credit card debt over a long period of time and had to have more income quickly.

He told me he wanted to tell me about his situation, but his father-in-law convinced him not to take the risk thinking I might terminate him on the spot. I explained to him the consequences of him not telling me. Had I known, I might have been able to help him. And the stress Susan went through would not have been necessary since his departure would resolve the budget issue.

We ended up asking Susan to stay, which she was glad to do, but the whole scenario created chaos for the company that had hired her. It also created chaos for Susan and us.

You can see how desire played into this chaotic scenario—Tom's desire to ease the stress of his debt and the family pressure it created, Tom's desire to reduce risk by not telling me, Susan's desire to stay, and my stress of having to ask Susan to leave.

> ## This chaos occurred because Tom's fears were stronger than his trust in me.

The point of this story is not to judge anyone's decision. (A biblical principle is that when we judge others, we have put ourselves in the place of God and only add to the problem of relating to others.) The point of the story is that this chaos occurred because Tom's fears were stronger than his trust in me. I have responsibility because I did not spend enough time getting to know about Tom's situation. This illustrates the importance of the prior chapter. If I had paid enough attention to Tom's situation could we have addressed this issue in a better way? I will never know. But the principle is that the more you care about people, the better leader you will be.

Now for another example involving my own shortsightedness.

An Authoritarian Boss

Early in my career, I was so driven that I would get angry when people gave me feedback that differed from my view. The root of the anger was twofold: (1) perceived lack of respect for me and (2) obstruction of my goals. My arrogant mind couldn't believe that someone had a better idea. I knew what was best. And second, I saw disagreement as slowing the process down. Let's get on with it.

It did not take long to learn that my anger caused people around me to shut down. Rather than endure my wrath, they would suppress

> Rather than endure my wrath, they would suppress information that might have helped if I had been willing to listen.

> If I invest in relationships with my people, those bonds help them tolerate and forgive my errant behavior.

information that might have helped if I had been willing to listen. These are hard behaviors to face and change.

But if we don't, the outcome is that poor decisions are made without all the information needed. And it leads to destructive conversations outside the meeting. So disgruntlement sets in with negative, resentful, and probably accurate assessments about the boss's bad decision-making.

I admit I am still pretty driven and sometimes violate my own standards of openness. I say things that could create barriers and shut down others. But here is where caring for people helps. If I invest in relationships with my people, those bonds help them tolerate and forgive my errant behavior. Knowing my weakness, I tell people around me frequently that I want their input even when I act like I don't. Caring for people makes for a more resilient organization where our inevitable failures don't derail the teamwork.

Just as my personality affects my behavior, so it does with the people around you. Let's explore what to do about that.

Valuing Differences

Another barrier to openness and honesty is failing to recognize differences in personalities. Anyone who has raised children knows that from day one, each child is different. And they react to the same circumstances differently.

I recall one time when my firstborn son, at about nine months old, threw some food on the floor. I said "no" and tapped him on his hand with two fingers. He looked at me, scrunched up his face, and started crying.

Three years later, I had a repeat experience with our daughter. She threw food on the floor; I tapped her hand. She looked me straight in the eye and hit my hand instead. No crying, no anger, just determination.

The people on your team are different, too, and you have to figure out how to leverage those differences. These difference are valuable.

Behavioral Assessment Tools   One suggestion for developing your ability to understand those natural preferences in yourself and others is using personality assessments. Disclaimer: I am not advocating that anyone make any important decisions based on any personality assessment tool. The human mind is too complex to model accurately.

However, assessments are tools to raise awareness of the differences in people and what motivates them. Think of them as a framework for *discussing* differences rather than accurately *defining* them.

> Assessments are tools to raise awareness of the differences in people and what motivates them.

Nothing replaces just sitting down and talking with others. But having a framework to organize your learning will speed the process. The following are some popular personality assessment tools. There are hundreds more. The primary value gained is not in which tool you choose; it is whether you use it that matters.

- The Myer-Briggs Type Indicator (MBTI);
- DISC;
- Big 5 Personality;
- 16 personalities;
- StrengthsFinder;
- Clifton Strengths;
- Jung Personality.

The best way to learn is by doing, so I suggest you pick a tool that is easy to understand, quick to administer, and low cost enough that you can use it with all your team members. Adopting a common approach *throughout the organization* makes it easier for people to share learning and create a common language and culture that helps keep the reality of differences front and center.

The first assessment I used was a very high-quality instrument, but it was so expensive that clients could not use it broadly. Another instrument had hundreds of questions, which was not practical for many workers to take. Finally I realized a well-applied, basic instrument was more useful than the "perfect" instrument that was not practical to use broadly. Again, pick an assessment you will use with *everyone* in your organization.

To illustrate, let's use the DISC model. It is easy to remember, making it easier to apply while speaking with people. The DISC model is based on a range of preferences in two dimensions:

1. How people react to the environment—*act on* it or *react to* it; and

2. How people react to people—*open* or *cautious*.

Figure 15.2 shows this framework. No two people are exactly alike in where they fall on these two axes.

6D DISC Personality Assessment

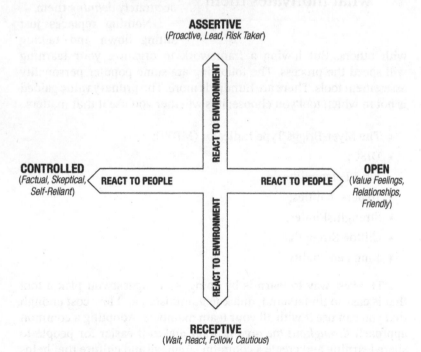

ASSERTIVE
(Proactive, Lead, Risk Taker)

REACT TO ENVIRONMENT

CONTROLLED
(Factual, Skeptical, Self-Reliant)

REACT TO PEOPLE

REACT TO PEOPLE

OPEN
(Value Feelings, Relationships, Friendly)

REACT TO ENVIRONMENT

RECEPTIVE
(Wait, React, Follow, Cautious)

FIGURE 15.2 DISC axes.
Source: LeadFirst.ai.

For example: if I wanted to hire someone in a cold-calling sales role, I would want to determine whether the person enjoys initiating action. Cold-calling depends on interrupting other people, and you get a lot of rejection. You need an internal drive to be that proactive. Otherwise, you will become overcome by the rejection. In DISC terms, this would be a combination of assertiveness to circumstances and openness to people.

However, if you are hiring someone who is taking an order from someone who has already decided to buy (inbound sales), you would want a person who enjoys reacting to a call and serving those people. In DISC terms, this would be a combination of being open to people and more receptive than assertive.

When people don't operate in their desires (motivations) enthusiasm wanes. It drains their energy, and it shows in the quantity and quality of work. However, the DISC model recognizes people can develop the ability to operate out of their natural tendencies. But it takes conscious effort and time to get comfortable.

With this framework in mind, you can quickly diagnose what is happening in interactions. For example, I worked with an executive team at a manufacturer to build a strategic plan. There was a lot of exciting discussion about the future. A few people tossed out ideas, and others joined in with reinforcement about what the future could bring.

But one person asked hard questions about what could go wrong, how much it would cost, etc. After hours of meeting, this tug-of-war created some tension.

Later on in the agenda was a DISC team-building session. When we got to that session, we discussed what makes people good at their jobs and their natural motivations. As you can guess, you want salespeople and strategy leaders to be risk-takers and assertive. But you want your financial function to be careful and controlled.

Without this balance, the organization will not be sustainable. On this team, the naysayer in the conversation was the CFO. When we described this dynamic from the DISC analysis, the tension lifted.

> They respected their differences instead of fighting them.

As the day progressed, people turned to the CFO and asked, "What do you think?" as a test of their thinking. They respected their differences instead of fighting them.

This illustrates why it is important to get at people's root motivations. It's key to get people in the right role and help them resolve conflict. If you understand the reasoning behind their actions, it is easier to reconcile the actions and get on a constructive path.

You want to build a culture where everyone knows that:

- Everyone is different in terms of natural desires and motivations.
- Actions flow out of those motivations.
- Different work requires different personality types.
- Understanding the reason behind the actions helps people work together more effectively and helps individuals think through their own actions.
- Everyone should become a student of desire!
- Again, success here does not depend on the tool you select. The ability to apply the tool is more important than the actual framework you choose.
- Now for another aspect of honesty and openness.

Agreed-upon Standards

One not so obvious issue that affects honesty and openness is defining and sharing standards that allow people to work together.

Let's say that I want to build a house. I engage an architect to come up with a plan. I give the builder the blueprints, which specify the dimensions and layout of the house. These are facts, and they are easily knowable. The blueprint is an "honest" representation of what I agreed to buy.

The only way ten carpenters can work together building my house is if they are using a common unit of measure. If one carpenter's tape measure uses twelve inches to mean a foot and another uses thirteen inches per foot, I will not be thrilled with the house they build. And frankly, they won't have much fun trying to build it. Nothing they do will fit together.

> If one carpenter's tape measure uses twelve inches to mean a foot and another uses thirteen inches per foot, I will not be thrilled with the house they build.

This simple example illustrates a couple of basic leadership considerations. Does your team know where to find the facts? And is the team all using the same standard for interpreting the facts as they pursue their purpose (build the house)?

Sometimes knowing the facts isn't even enough; read on.

Can't Accept the Facts

Another barrier to openness and honesty is the inability to *accept* the facts. In Chapter 1, we discussed the failed project that led to layoffs in our company in my early years as a CEO. That project went on for years, with missed deadlines and many red flags. But I was unwilling to face those facts.

I was taught as a youngster to never give up. Perseverance is a strength. But how do you recognize when to give up on one idea and move on to another? In my case, it was running out of cash—I was forced to accept the facts.

Sometimes I (you) get so focused that we just miss the truth. It can be determination as in my preceding case or it can be inattention. Let me explain.

Beyond Skin Deep

It is very easy to deceive ourselves that we are communicating. In my experience, words are a poor approximation for meaning. They are sometimes the best we have, but they are inadequate to reflect the depth of experience and meaning. For example, as a teenage boy, the first thing that came to my mind when I heard the word *intimacy* was sex. As you mature, you realize that open communication is far more intimate. Sexual lust exposes our skin; honest communication exposes our heart.

> Sexual lust exposes our skin; honest communication exposes our heart.

There is no greater vulnerability than sharing the fragile emotions and desires inside of us. Once shared, you can't take them back.

You become vulnerable since someone now knows something about you, and you are no longer in control of that information. You depend on the trust in the relationship. And perhaps that relationship could change. One sad example is when marriages break, and anger leads to betrayal of trust. This leads to future reluctance to be vulnerable.

> I mourn when I think of times when someone was trying to share something important with me, and I was too self-absorbed to realize what was happening.

I mourn when I think of times when someone was trying to share something important with me, and I was too self-absorbed to realize what was happening. Yet over time, I have learned to respect people who are trying to communicate with me. I work harder to *understand* what they are saying before I evaluate it. I believe it was Stephen Covey who said, "Being heard is the psychological equivalent of air." That sums up the significance of communication.

We are not doing this very well. Every employee survey from every client we have ever worked with lists communication as the top complaint. Somehow a fundamental need is not being met. Effective leaders must stay close enough to their team to uncover those situations before they grow into a larger problem.

Of the four boxes (Figure 15.3) of desire, reason, intention, and action, only actions are visible. The rest have to be uncovered with open communication.

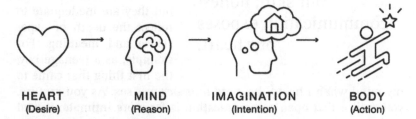

| HEART | MIND | IMAGINATION | BODY |
| (Desire) | (Reason) | (Intention) | (Action) |

FIGURE 15.3 Human architecture.
Source: LeadFirst.ai.

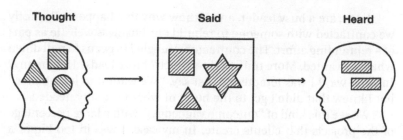

Thought   Said   Heard

FIGURE 15.4 Thought-said-heard.

It is no wonder that words are a poor approximation of meaning. We are trying to convey four-dimensional thoughts with two-dimensional words.

It is no wonder that words are a poor approximation of meaning. We are trying to convey four-dimensional thoughts with two-dimensional words. Figure 15.4 illustrates two potential challenges with communication. We are not great at saying what we mean. So the words don't fully express our thoughts. Listeners interpret our words according to their experience, not our intention.

And if saying what we mean wasn't challenging enough, let's move on to knowing what we mean.

Saying What We Mean Is Not Enough

There is also a more nuanced problem than saying what we mean. That problem is *knowing* what we mean. We are often lazy in defining what we want, even in our own mind.. A simple example is that when working with clients, a constant challenge is clearly stating project outcomes, being precise about what you really want a project to achieve

I, too, am a busy leader, and I know why this happens. Recently we contracted with someone to rebuild our business website as part of a rebranding effort. The contractor struggled to get us to nail down what we wanted. More traffic? How much? More leads? How many? In what way? I was tempted to just say, "We want it to look better," but I knew that didn't get to the heart of what we really needed.

We see this kind of "outcome vagueness" with a large percentage of the projects that clients create. In my case, I was in too big of a hurry to figure out what I needed from this project. Fortunately, the project manager would not let me get away with it.

> Lack of clarity delegates the definition of what success is to someone else.... It's strange that we have time to do the project over again but don't have time to do it right the first time.

> Lack of clarity causes a loss of motivation and innovation. Have you ever worked on a project that accomplished nothing? How did you feel?

Lack of clarity delegates the definition of what success is to someone else. Yet when you get the result, you are disappointed that it wasn't what you wanted. It's strange that we have time to do the project over again but don't have time to do it right the first time.

Being clear in communication is hard work, but people want it desperately. Why? Because they have a deep desire to "win." If we can't explain what we want, those around us don't understand what "winning" means. Lack of clarity causes a loss of motivation and innovation. Have you ever worked on a project that accomplished nothing? How did you feel?

As Figure 15.4 shows, sending a message is only part of the problem. The other part is verifying that understanding is achieved. Was the message received accurately?

In *The 7 Habits of Highly Effective People*, Stephen Covey advocates a simple process to communicate effectively. He proposes that when someone explains something to you, listen carefully and restate what you heard in your own words until the sender confirms you understood accurately. This technique requires both parties to listen well.

Let's wrap up with a few tips.

Getting Real—Eight Tips

- When you lose your temper, stop and apologize immediately.
- Encourage "constructive conflict." Patrick Lencioni, author of *The Five Dysfunctions of a Team*, points out that a lack of conflict also leads to poor commitment to decisions. He writes:

  A lack of healthy conflict is a problem because it ensures the third dysfunction of a team: lack of commitment. Without having aired their opinions in the course of passionate and open debate, team members rarely, if ever, buy in and commit to decisions, though they may feign agreement during meetings.

  Lencioni, Patrick M. The Five Dysfunctions of a Team *(J-B Lencioni Series) (pp. 188–189). Wiley. Kindle Edition.*

- Involve everyone in conversations. Direct some questions to those who are less likely to speak up. If necessary, get input in one-on-one meetings from those who seem reluctant about a particular topic. In the next chapter we introduce the "Gordian" exercise, which is a process that helps achieve this.
- Address chronic destructive behavioral problems. No one is so valuable that team-damaging behavior can be justified. Address such behaviors promptly.
- Use team surveys to build awareness of group performance. Create benchmarks and monitor progress frequently, at least quarterly. Accountability helps the natural tendency to lapse into bad habits again.
- Use tools such as multi-rater feedback, which provides anonymous feedback from a group of people to an individual. It is more difficult to reject input when multiple people are saying the same thing.

- Incorporate evaluation of this value into performance reviews and other one-to-one interactions. Be clear that you are serious about this.
- Practice what you preach. People will do as you do, not what you say.

Building a high-trust culture sets up the next stage of engagement behaviors: building oneness, which is covered in the next chapter. First some additional biblical insights about openness and honesty.

Biblical Insights for Wise Living

- "Better is a poor man who walks in his integrity than a rich man who is crooked in his ways" (Proverbs 28:6).
- "The integrity of the upright guides them, but the crookedness of the treacherous destroys them" (Proverbs 11:3).
- "One who is faithful in a very little is also faithful in much, and one who is dishonest in a very little is also dishonest in much" (Luke 16:10).
- "Lying lips are an abomination to the LORD, but those who act faithfully are his delight" (Proverbs 12:22).
- "Whoever walks in integrity walks securely, but he who makes his ways crooked will be found out" (Proverbs 10:9).
- "A false balance is an abomination to the LORD, but a just weight is his delight" (Proverbs 11:1).
- "Therefore, having put away falsehood, let each one of you speak the truth with his neighbor, for we are members one of another" (Ephesians 4:25).
- "A dishonest man spreads strife, and a whisperer separates close friends" (Proverbs 16:28).
- "One who is faithful in a very little is also faithful in much, and one who is dishonest in a very little is also dishonest in much" (Luke 16:10).

CHAPTER 16

Someone Who Builds Oneness

...the whole body, joined and held together by every joint with which it is equipped, when each part is working properly, makes the body grow so that it builds itself up in love.

Ephesians 4

B y now, I hope you are starting to see how the pieces in this book fit together—how it is that we overcome chaos. Let's reconstruct the logic of doing so:

- Know that people are created to win. They not only want to win—they need to win. It is one of our deepest human needs.

- Work together. We can't attain most of the things we want by ourselves. We have to figure out how to work together, yet our individual desires fight us.

- Expect difficulty. Working together is always a challenge, and it always will be. The more the community grows, the more complex our communication and coordination tasks become. This means we have to leverage people and managerial processes to manage this complexity. Since the laws of physics don't apply to human behavior, it is more difficult to scale the number of people in a building than it is the buildings they occupy.

- Relationships come first. The primary bonding force for humans is the strength of our relationships, the intangible sense of people caring about us and us them and a mutual caring about shared purposes. This creates trust.

- Purpose is key. For people to win in a group setting, they need to see how they contribute to the team's purpose. This, too, requires complete honesty and openness.

> The primary bonding force for humans is the strength of our relationships, the intangible sense of people caring about us and us them.

In this chapter we will dig deeper on how to turn a group of individuals into a unified team. Building oneness is the third stage in the people engagement model (Figure 16.1).

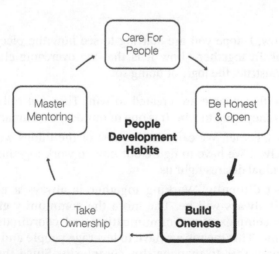

FIGURE 16.1 People engagement—oneness.

The Power of One

The whole Bible, from beginning to end, conveys the idea that having dominion means building things, putting together the chaos of raw materials and relationships all to accomplish some purpose. That is what you are designed for. We often use the term *building oneness* when referring to the process of integrating these pieces. There are frequent illustrations of this important concept in the biblical narrative.

Revisiting Chapter 5, the Bible speaks of God as "one" existing as three "persons"—the Father, the Son, and the Holy Spirit. The marriage of a man and woman is spoken of as becoming "one." God's image is expressed as a man and woman together, not individually but collectively. The Church is also spoken of as "one."

This is not unusual. We speak of a group of separate individuals that function together as a unit. Sports teams win and lose as one, and so do businesses, orchestras, and families.

> Building oneness inside yourself is another way to describe self-leadership.

Forming oneness is a two-step process. First, within the individual, all four attributes we described in Part 1—purpose, reason, intention, and action (Figure 16.2)—have to be aligned. Second, the individuals in a team have to align with a shared purpose.

Building oneness inside yourself is another way to describe self-leadership. Building it among others is group leadership. Although achievement of oneness is never complete, the Bible states that the upside is unlimited in terms of benefits.

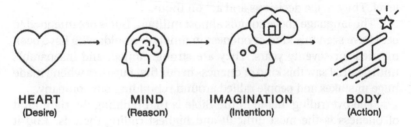

HEART **MIND** **IMAGINATION** **BODY**
(Desire) (Reason) (Intention) (Action)

FIGURE 16.2 Human architecture.

This is another reminder that our challenge isn't our capability to create; it's our capability to integrate or become "one."

God states in the story of the tower of Babel that when people communicate together as one, they can accomplish anything. The quote is worth rereading: "Behold, they are *one* people, and they have all *one* language, and this is only the beginning of what they will do. And *nothing* that they propose to do will now be impossible for them." This is another reminder that our challenge isn't our capability to create; it's our capability to integrate or become "one" as stated in this verse.

What Does "Oneness" Look Like?

You know it when you see it. Someone in the boxing world is thought to have coined the phrase "lean, mean fighting machine." Regardless of origin, it conveys the essence of a kind of oneness that stands out when you are around it. Some of the obvious attributes of people on a team who are "one":

They have a clear purpose as a starting point.

They are united around that purpose. They stand together. Whatever differences they have, they are secondary to their purpose.

They are inseparable and unstoppable—relentless in their pursuit. They are resilient and tough and learn from mistakes.

They have the right people on the team, and each knows their role.

They have strong leadership both at the individual and the team level. They make decisions and act on them.

The language above sounds almost militant. But is not intended to be. I have seen this kind of oneness in ninety-year-olds who have been married for seventy years. They are strong, united, and inseparable until death. I saw this kind of oneness in our first business when I made huge mistakes and people rallied around rebuilding our company.

The overriding theme in the Bible is that building the right kind of oneness is the most difficult and highest calling there is. And it comes at a high price. Oneness with God Himself came at the price paid on Calvary Hill two thousand years ago. Oneness in friendships

> The overriding theme in the Bible is that building the right kind of oneness is the most difficult and highest calling there is. And it comes at a high price.

comes at the cost of openness, forgiveness, and time invested. And oneness in organizations comes at the high cost of forming shared purpose and learning how to work together toward that purpose.

Learning to do just that is the purpose of this book. The only way you can overcome chaos is uniting people around shared purpose.

Do I have all the answers on how to do this? Of course not. But I do have decades of learning (read mistakes) from the business world and I want to share a few tips.

Not for Wimps

Tip 1: Fight for It

The group leader must recognize the need for oneness and be willing to fight for it. Set expectations that everyone will learn how to treat each other with care and respect and work together. No exceptions.

> Divisive behaviors have to be constructively but firmly called out and good behaviors reinforced.

Without achieving this behavior nothing else will last. Day-to-day interactions have to reinforce this priority. Divisive behaviors have to be constructively but firmly called out and good behaviors reinforced.

Tip 2: Clarify Purpose Relentlessly

Conquering chaos and building teams all start with purpose. Purpose is the charter for the team. To instill purpose, you must understand two dimensions. First, the leader must understand the organization's strategy and convey it to the team. Building understanding can't be done with one presentation. Understanding must be reinforced continually using examples from day-to-day work.

Second, the team has to understand its own strategy and decompose that into its individual roles. This also requires ongoing reinforcement.

> The only problem is that these things rarely happen. If you don't believe me, go to any department in your organization and ask the leader to explain the company strategy.

This might sound so obvious that it's boring. The only problem is that these things rarely happen. If you don't believe me, go to any department in your organization and ask the leader to explain the company strategy. Then, ask one of the team members to explain their department strategy and how it fits in to the organization's overall strategy.

Tip 3: Explore "How" Together

The leader owns the mission of the group and the broad strategies for fulfilling the mission. That implies some setting of big-picture goals and priorities. But the group needs to have a say in how those goals are met.

This is where honesty, or should I say brutal honesty, needs to occur. The group must discuss openly how to reach the goals—and even question the goals if needed. Different approaches need to be debated thoroughly. This is how to get the best solutions.

> I admit that I still don't look forward to that process on the front end. Deep down I want my plans to be right without input.

After decades in business, I am still surprised that when I go into a meeting and propose something, my plans improve when I listen to others. I admit that I still don't look forward to that process on the front end. Deep down I want my plans to be right without input. But experience has taught me that I am a fool if I don't invite people to examine my ideas.

The reason for this is obvious. It is impossible for any individual to know all of what others know. They experience things you never will. So it makes sense when forming decisions to gather input. As Solomon stated, "Without counsel plans fail, but with many advisers they succeed" (Proverbs 15).

Tip 4: Get Honest Commitment

The ultimate definition of oneness is not polite conversation. It is a hard-core commitment to do what it takes to reach shared goals. People on the team have to detect weak commitment and get to the bottom of any barriers. The analogy that comes to mind is my father warning me to never paint something that is rusted. He taught me to scrape and brush until the metal was completely free of rust and corrosion *before* painting. I can hear still him say, "Don't stop until you get to bare metal." Otherwise the paint will not last. So it is with building a unified team. You cannot paint over corrosion, you must resolve conflict and concerns to build teamwork.

It is a tough, hard-fought battle both inside you and with your group, but as people struggle to achieve this deep commitment, they experience the joy of oneness. The journey is difficult, but there is nothing like fighting that battle together.

Tip 5: Stay in Synch

The only thing you can be sure of when creating a plan is that it is not right. Things change, and they change fast. The real purpose of planning is to create a deeper understanding of purpose within the team. It is out of that understanding that people can work together.

> The only thing you can be sure of when creating a plan is that it is not right. Things change, and they change fast.

As new information flows in, adjustments have to be made. Teams need a way to stay on the same page, process the latest feedback, and quickly adjust. In the football sports analogy, you build a multi-year personnel plan, a season plan, a game plan, call a play in the huddle, and call an audible at the line of scrimmage. Individual players react to the play as it develops, including scrambling to change the play after it has started.

Similarly, business teams also need a system of communication and strategy. Part 2 laid out many best practices that range from strategic planning to quarterly, weekly, and even daily realignment. But since every team is different, communication methods must be tailored to each team. Even though leaders know this, they often don't get it done. Information is the oxygen that teams run on. Without it they quickly become weak and disoriented.

> Information is the oxygen that teams run on. Without it they quickly become weak and disoriented.

All the preceding tips are woven into the processes and principles throughout the book. Now let's go to the opposite extreme and talk about what not to do.

To Kill Teamwork Do This

Unfortunately because I have the years of experience to give you tips about what works, I have also made enough mistakes to be able to tell you with full authority what does *not* work

As you design your leadership and management approach do the following if you want to kill teamwork:

1. Use Force
- There are a variety of ways to coerce people. You may force people into choices they don't want if you pay them enough, but if the work does not align with their desires, you won't get the same contribution. This is not rebellion; it is a fact of human need. When we are in our "zone," we contribute more. We have more energy, more

> ...but if the work does not align with their desires, you won't get the same contribution. This is not rebellion....

insight, and are easier to interact with. The role of leaders is not to force but find the natural alignment.

2. Treat Everyone the Same

- One-size-fits-all systems don't work, either. Some personality types need more structure and direction. Others need more freedom. Some want to work uninterrupted; others get energy from interacting with others. Leaders have to study people and optimize team alignment to strategy.

3. Don't Change

- Static, inflexible systems don't work. The right approach today won't work tomorrow. Why? Because plans change, people change, customers change, organizations change. The world changes. Nothing stays the same, ever.

A word of caution. Don't interpret the preceding items to mean that everyone gets to do their own thing. Oneness is the opposite of that. A leader's role is to facilitate the formulation of purpose and the fitting of people together around shared purpose to achieve what no one individual could achieve. Sometimes that means moving people around on the team or even off the team. Leaders have to make building oneness their top priority and do whatever it takes to protect it.

> Don't interpret the preceding items to mean that everyone gets to do their own thing. Oneness is the opposite of that.

Moving on from what doesn't work, I want to share a process that does.

Gordian™ Problem Solving

Years ago a business associate, Steven Dennis of Smith, Dennis and Gaylord, shared with me an exercise for group prioritization setting. He called it the "100 Point Exercise." There are many similar approaches, but the idea is to have a group brainstorm on solutions to some problem and then give people one hundred points each, which they can allocate as votes among the ideas.

This can be done with Post-it® notes or many other ways. The principle behind the exercise is to get everyone's ideas on the table *and* to realize you can't do everything, so the one hundred points reflect limited resources. By tallying the votes you cut through the chaos and surface the top solution candidates using the collective wisdom of the group.

The process works amazingly well. At Solomon Software we had an annual gathering of our business partners, and one particular year there were two thousand people gathered in Cincinnati. As part of this event we had a breakout session with about thirty delegates of our partner channel who provided advice on our software development priorities. As CEO I joined this meeting in progress, and there was a great deal of lively conversation and some of it pretty heated discussion about what should be the priorities and why. The wall was covered with lists of suggestions. To get the meeting under control, one of our leaders introduced the one hundred Point Exercise, and within thirty minutes we had a top-ten list, that the group felt good about. It really does help groups dialogue effectively.

Over the years, however, this process has evolved into what we call the Gordian Problem Solving™ approach. The name "Gordian" is a reference to Greek mythology where a former Phrygian king located in Gordium, in Asia Minor, had tied his ox cart to a pole with a very complex knot. A seer predicted that whoever would untie that knot would become the ruler of all Asia. Legend has it that Alexander the Great when confronted with this problem pulled out his sword and with a single slice cut it in two.

> "Slicing through a Gordian knot" has become a metaphor for attacking a difficult problem in a new way, approaching it from a different angle.

"Slicing through a Gordian knot" has become a metaphor for attacking a difficult problem in a new way, approaching it from a different angle. Alexander, unlike predecessors who had failed, chose to not untie the knot but cut through it.

The Gordian process—as we call it—is simple, but the results are profound. Here are the steps:

1. State clearly the problem you are trying to solve. Put it in the form of a question. An example from Chapter 1 of this book is

"How can we build and deploy a Windows version of our product within two years using only five people?"

2. Get the right people in the room to tackle this problem. They should represent a broad perspective of disciplines—marketing, engineering, finance, project management, design, production, quality, customer service, sales. You want people who see things from a different angle.

3. Do real brainstorming. Real brainstorming pushes people to state ideas quickly without thinking about feasibility. Often using a timer stops the temptation to evaluate. The point of brainstorming is to break free of siloed constraints. The power of brainstorming is that my weird idea that is no good may trigger your weird idea that is a breakthrough.

4. After the new ideas have been exhausted, have everyone vote privately. Each person is given a limited number of votes, so they are forced to prioritize and evaluate. The key is that they think through the problem from their own perspective.

5. After everyone has voted, everyone explains their vote without debate. Others can ask clarifying questions but they cannot attack ideas. Why? Because as was discussed in the prior chapter you want to build a culture of openness. You need everyone to feel free to speak up. In DISC terminology it is easy for some personalities to defend their ideas, for others it is not. Optimal solutions and breakthroughs occur when people listen to each other.

6. After everyone has had their turn to explain their reasoning, the group votes again. Why? Because when people hear what someone outside their area of expertise has to say they almost always learn something that changes their perspective on what the best solution is.

7. After people vote again, you review the results again. The objective is not to always come up with agreement on *the* solution. The objective is get clear understanding of the trade-offs and the rationale for the top couple of solutions. This exercise does not replace the responsibility of the decision-maker to make the final call.

We have used this exercise more than five thousand times over the past twenty years. More than 90% of the time people come out of the meeting energized and on the same page about clarity of direction.

So why does this work? First, it demonstrates that you care enough about every person in the room that you want to hear their input. (This is the subject of Chapter 14.) Next, it creates an environment where the dominant personalities are controlled so that

> So why does this work? First, it demonstrates that you care enough about every person in the room that you want to hear their input.

everyone is heard. The quiet personalities learn to speak up. The dominant personalities learn to listen. (This is the subject of Chapter 15.) Third, it recognizes the value of different perspectives. Someone in finance looks at the world differently from someone in sales. We need each other to get the whole picture.

Since we have done this so many times, we have found that we can save time using software to capture the ideas and do the voting. This allows the process to work remotely or in an off-line (asynchronous) approach. As an encouragement to those who have made it this far in the book, we have created an app that appears in the Apple and Android stores. You can get it for free using the promo code "chaos." (See Appendix for more information.)

A House Divided

Before we close this chapter, consider this insight from Jesus as He was confronting those who were against Him and what He was trying to do. "Every kingdom divided against itself is laid waste, and no city or house divided against itself will stand" (Matthew 12).

> For us mortals it is difficult to be clear about purpose and make sure it is aligned. It is even more difficult to keep everyone on the same page moving toward that purpose.

When Jesus said this, he was responding to those who interpreted His actions as being against His own stated purpose. There are a couple of leadership lessons in this quote. First, as leaders, our decisions have to align with our purpose. As Jesus says, a lack of unity around purpose will not stand. Jesus knew the importance of creating oneness within a team. For us mortals it is difficult to be clear about purpose and make sure it is aligned. It is even more difficult to keep everyone on the same page moving toward that purpose. But that's what leaders must do.

The second lesson is that some people will not understand your decisions and attempt to use your own actions against you. A good example of this are those times when you need to end the relationship with an employee. People may say, "I thought you said you cared about people. How can you do this?"

The answer is that it there is no inconsistency. If I care about someone, I want what's best for them. Continuing to employ them in work where they can't succeed is not what's best for them or for the team they work with. If they can't win within our organization, I am lying to them to allow them to continue. That is not love.

> If they can't win within our organization, I am lying to them to allow them to continue. That is not love.

I close this chapter with a reminder that a commitment to oneness is not an easy road. Jesus Himself was misunderstood to the point that He was killed. And His purpose was to help the very people who killed Him. It is the ultimate example of leadership and love.

In the next chapter, we will move on from building oneness to taking ownership of our commitments.

Additional Wisdom about Oneness, Teamwork, and Unity

- "Two are better than one, because they have a good return for their labor: If either of them falls down, one can help the other up. But pity anyone who falls and has no one to help them up" (Ecclesiastes 4:9).
- "Each of you should use whatever gift you have received to serve others, as faithful stewards of God's grace in its various forms" (1 Peter 4:10).

- "For which of you, desiring to build a tower, does not first sit down and count the cost, whether he has enough to complete it?" (Luke 14:28).

- "Behold, how good and pleasant it is when brothers dwell in unity!" (Psalms 133:1).

- "I appeal to you, brothers, by the name of our Lord Jesus Christ, that all of you agree, and that there be no divisions among you, but that you be united in the same mind and the same judgment" (1 Corinthians 1:10).

- "And above all these put on love, which binds everything together in perfect harmony" (Colossians 3:14).

- "Live in harmony with one another. Do not be haughty, but associate with the lowly. Never be wise in your own sight" (Romans 12:16).

- "Do nothing from selfish ambition or conceit, but in humility count others more significant than yourselves" (Philippians 2:3).

CHAPTER 17

Takes Ownership

...Don't just obey like people pleasers when they are watching. Instead, obey with the single motivation of fearing the Lord.

Colossians 3 (CEBA)

In this chapter, we will explore how to develop "ownership" for yourself and for your team. In the people engagement model (Figure 17.1), take ownership follows build oneness for a very important reason. The "build oneness" phase is where groups become united around team goals and at the same time begin to understand their own individual role in pursuit of those goals. Without that understanding, real ownership can't take place.

So what does ownership mean? I propose five traits.

Trait 1: Team Results Come First

The first and most important understanding is that the team wins and loses as a team. Team goals come first.

Like any team, there are team goals and individual responsibilities. Each person must understand the play being called and their part in that play. But they also have to subordinate their individual goals to the goals of the team.

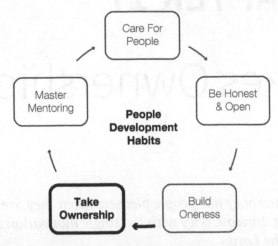

FIGURE 17.1 People engagement model—take ownership.

This is exactly why the previous step of building "oneness" is so important. In it, everyone comes to understand what "one" means—the game we are playing and what winning means for the team.

The mindset of the team members has to be one of sacrificing their individual goals when needed to attain the team goals. The alternative mindset of "I did my part, and you didn't" is another type of cancer that will destroy the team.

> The mindset of the team members has to be one of sacrificing their individual goals when needed to attain the team goals.

Let's revisit the orchestra example in Chapter 7. It perfectly illustrates the power of oneness. Musicians are highly creative people and often want to express themselves in unique ways. This could lead to a strong desire to do one's own thing. Yet playing in an orchestra is demonstrates the synergy that occurs when subjecting one's individual freedom to fit a very precise role. It takes a lifetime of learning and preparation and lots of practice, and the result is magnificent.

The musicians I know don't struggle to commit. They want to experience what *only* the team can produce. They love it. That illustrates what ownership means. It is a combination of wanting to be part of a whole and putting your all into achieving team results.

This commitment to the team leads to the next healthy trait.

Trait 2: Results *and* Behaviors Matter

Teams understand that it is better to lose a game than lose the team. If the team is destroyed, all games will be lost.

As a reminder, a culture of openness and trust is the foundation on which teamwork is built. The group has to view protecting the culture as just as important as achieving business goals. The goals may be more *urgent*, but the teamwork culture is more *important* long term.

This may be the most difficult aspect of ownership. Team members must check their ego "at the door" so the team can honestly diagnose what is working and what is not. This requires a commitment to the team that exceeds commitment to self.

It can mean calling someone out whose behavior and attitude is destructive to the team—or calling someone out who is not taking responsibility for goals seriously. This does not mean squashing dissenting views; it means the opposite. It means getting critical issues on the table with the motive of improving the team. It doesn't mean self-gratification.

This all sounds good in theory, but can easily feel like we are under attack as this kind of openness occurs. This is why trusted relationships are necessary to provide the resilience to withstand constructive disagreement.

> They have polite, surface-level dialogue about issues that are holding them back. Then the deeper dialogue takes place outside the room, behind people's back.

The alternative is that organizations never get to this level of trust. They have polite, surface-level dialogue about issues that are holding them back. Then the deeper dialogue takes place outside the room, behind people's back. The result is no resolution of the root cause and a culture of resentment and distrust. It is a destructive cycle that kills progress.

A logical outcome of accountability and openness is a recognition of gaps in team capability. Read on.

Trait 3: Capability Gaps Are Closed

Effective teams face up to their skill set honestly. They self-assess whether they have what it takes for their mission.

This can be personally challenging for individuals on the team who may overestimate their own capability. As we keep repeating, facing the facts takes openness, honesty, and trust.

The best performing teams attempt to think ahead and identify future gaps in time to do something about it either through training or team structure. This look ahead is described in Chapters 10 and 13 as a planning best practice. The more teams anticipate future needs, the more proactive they can be at plugging gaps and reducing the cost of those gaps. As before, if there is no openness to identify the gaps, they just get larger, and the whole team pays the price.

The bottom line is that this kind of ownership requires the discipline to not just deal with the *urgent* goals of the day but to deal with the *important* goals that will prepare the team for the future.

Trait 4: Conflict Is Expected and Managed

Face it, the uniqueness of humans makes conflict inevitable. The first step in managing conflict effectively is to expect it, to realize that it is normal, and prepare to manage it proactively.

The Bible alludes to this principle:

Where there are no oxen, the manger is clean, but abundant crops come by the strength of the ox.

Proverbs 14

> **If you want the benefit of the ox, you have to be prepared to do the shoveling of the crap that goes with it.**

> **Conflicts are going to occur, and you should not think of them as avoidable.**

As a farm boy, I know what a mess is created by livestock in their living quarters. Dare I say that manure stinks and has to be shoveled out by hand (at least in my day). But if you want the benefit of the ox, you have to be prepared to do the shoveling of the crap that goes with it. You can't have it both ways.

So it is with leadership. Conflicts are going to occur, and you should not think of them as avoidable. The apostle Paul tells the Church at Corinth that "there must, in fact, be divisions among you, so that those of you who are approved may be evident" (2 Corinthians 8). He is making the same point that differences are required to sort out what is the best answer.

Avoiding differences or sweeping conflict under the rug just makes it surface later in other, larger ways. Great teams have to be embrace conflict in real time and in healthy ways.

The following is an approach that has worked for me in managing conflict:

- Talk to the parties of the conflict individually and listen carefully to what the issues are.

- Get the parties together and make sure they know you will not tolerate this issue not being resolved. You will not sacrifice the team's oneness over their disagreement.

- Make sure all the issues raised by both parties are on the table. Frequently, when two different parties explain their issues, they are able to identify misunderstandings and resolve the issues then and there.

- I have found it useful in some situations to use DISC assessments as a tool to help people see communication differences that explain some of the tension that naturally occurs among different communication styles.

- If all else fails and the two can't come up a solution, you, as the leader, will have to impose a solution. That solution could range from mandatory change in behavior or attitude to reassignment or separation. I repeat, nothing can be put ahead of the unity of the team. No one is above that.

To illustrate this process, I share my experience as a coach in a large nonprofit organization. I was asked to evaluate a department that was not performing well. As I started asking questions, it quickly became clear that the problem was caused by two people who fought constantly and couldn't get along. Their relationship had spilled over to the whole team.

They would not discuss their reasons with each other. But in my drill down, one party shared that his spouse told him that the other person had made an inappropriate comment to that spouse. In a joint meeting, the parties were unwilling to get the issue out in the open, and as a facilitator, I brought it into the open.

The accused party denied it had happened and did not know it was the basis of the animosity. Here, the damage and trust issues were so deep they were unreconcilable, and one party left. Was this a success in terms of reconciliation? No. Was it a success in addressing the conflict, so it didn't affect the team? Yes.

As leaders, it is your responsibility to see that these kinds of issues are resolved promptly one way or another.

A specific kind of conflict that can arise in teams is poor performance. Read on.

Trait 5: Poor Performance Is Addressed Proactively

When an individual is not performing at acceptable levels it must be addressed promptly. Not doing so is being dishonest with the individual and breaks trust with the team. Such issues unaddressed long enough and frequently enough eventually destroy the unity of a team. The breakdown compounds, performance gets worse, and you have a problem that is an order of magnitude more difficult to solve.

It is understandable why performance is not addressed promptly. First, of all a leader has to notice the poor performance. If they do not have clear plans in place and are not communicating one-on-one, the team may see the issues long before the manager. Second, once the leader recognizes the problem, the root cause(s) are not easy to diagnose. Are there external factors at work? Training issues? Aptitude issues? Attitude issues? Or hidden motivational issues? Team conflict?

The complexity of the factors involved plus the reluctance to talk openly about the situation leads to understandable but unwise delay. However, if you have been following the other engagement best practices of caring about people and build high trust relationships, you have the foundation upon which to diagnose and address issues with integrity.

Following are a few checklist items to guide the diagnosis process. However, this checklist only works if you and the individual have an open dialogue and are focused on the same goal: aligning the individual's strengths with the organization's needs.

If those two don't align, neither party can "win" in the long run. In that case, you must address the misalignment constructively and promptly. Allowing the misalignment to continue will only create more chaos.

Following are a few questions to consider as you work through your diagnosis:

- Have you had an open conversation with the individual that clearly states the concern?
- Have you allowed them to express their own understanding of their performance? How well do *they* think they are doing? And

why do they believe that? Is there a misunderstanding about their job?

- Is there a difference in understanding? How can that difference be reconciled? What are the facts?
- Are there other contributing factors that need to be resolved? Dependencies on others? Process problems?
- Is there an openness to the input? What are the options for improvement? Training? Mentoring?
- If performance is not resolved, what are the options? Transfer? Time to find another job? Is there an understanding of this person's strengths and ideas for work that fits who they are?

The preceding checklist suggests no radical new ideas. What it promotes is an attitude of respect and openness. When non-performance is not addressed, it creates fear of the unknown for the employee. They usually know before you do that they are not performing well. Getting issues on the table reduces that fear and creates the best opportunities to address the issues successfully. This is referred to in the Bible as "speaking the truth in love." As pointed out in Chapter 14, motives matter. If you have built the foundation of a strong relationship, you will be more effective in getting to the best resolution for non-performance.

> They usually know before you do that they are not performing well.

As group leaders, it is our role to lead this process. We must be firm about getting our employees' performance to where it needs to be or finding a fit either in the organization or outside at another organization.

There are always people in their life journey who are bitter and difficult to work with. You cannot control how they react to you, but you can have the integrity of purpose as a leader to help people find fulfillment in their work. If that can't happen, you must require that they move on. Doing so requires a belief that moving on will get them another step closer to finding their spot in life. This can be a tough love situation where the individual may strongly disagree with you.

The final chapter will take us into the most rewarding part of leadership: building difference makers through mentoring.

Additional Wisdom about Taking Ownership:

- "Arise, for it is your task, and we are with you; be strong and do it" (Ezra 10:4).
- "For each will have to bear his own load" (Galatians 6:5).
- "Therefore encourage one another and build one another up, just as you are doing" (1 Thessalonians 5:11).
- "And let us consider how we may spur one another on toward love and good deeds, not giving up meeting together, as some are in the habit of doing, but encouraging one another..." (Hebrews 10:24).
- "So whoever knows the right thing to do and fails to do it, for him it is sin [missing the mark]" (James 4:17).
- "One who is faithful in a very little is also faithful in much, and one who is dishonest in a very little is also dishonest in much" (Luke 16:10–12).
- "Therefore, having put away falsehood, let each one of you speak the truth with his neighbor, for we are members one of another" (Ephesians 4:25).
- "The point is this: whoever sows sparingly will also reap sparingly, and whoever sows bountifully will also reap bountifully" (2 Corinthians 9:6–7).
- "Whatever you do, work heartily, as for the Lord and not for men" (Colossians 3:23).
- "Moreover, it is required of stewards that they be found faithful" (1 Corinthians 4:2).

CHAPTER 18

Someone Who Masters Mentoring

*With upright heart he shepherded them
and guided them with his skillful hand.*

Psalm 78

The purpose of this chapter is a little like chocolate cake. (I am a huge fan of Bill Knapp's chocolate cake, and Cheesecake Factory cake is right up there too.) But consider this. The ingredients of a chocolate cake are flour, sugar, baking soda, salt, and chocolate. Yet none of those ingredients by themselves predict the taste and experience of eating a piece of that cake. Like the delicious melting of cake in your mouth, there is mystery and surprise when you learn and follow biblical principles in life. The abundance is unexpectedly good and beyond any individual ingredient.

> Like the delicious melting of cake in your mouth, there is mystery and surprise when you learn and follow biblical principles in life.

In this chapter, mentoring people to grow into their potential is the cake, and the principles used are the

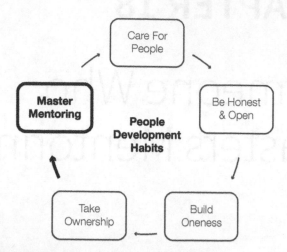

FIGURE 18.1   People engagement model—mentoring.

ingredients (Figure 18.1). The mixing of these ingredients is what the Bible refers to as wisdom. As we learned in Chapter 5, God created wisdom first.

Master mentoring is the last step in the behavior habits cycle that builds employee engagement. In the Bible, another word for mentoring is *discipleship*. In means to transfer learning to someone else through experiential training. It conveys the idea of learning as you go, working alongside of someone similar to the apprentice/craftsman model. *Being* a disciple conveys a commitment to *learning from* another disciple.

In the Bible, mentoring usually conveys the idea of training someone to the point of maturity where they can train someone else. In other words, you are not really a disciple until you have discipled someone else who has discipled someone. It is a high standard of mastery.

Why should you aspire to this kind of mentorship? First, it is deeply satisfying. We are built to help others learn and grow. Second, it helps the mentor learn faster. Teaching others teaches you. Third, organizations are overtaken by chaos if they can't reproduce leaders faster than they are growing. Mentoring is the proven way to maintain a culture, and building and maintaining a culture is how you change the world.

Changing the World

You don't change the world (or at least your part of the world) by doing things for people that they should do for themselves. This is a deception. Instead you equip and challenge people to grow into their roles and support them as they do so.

> You don't change the world (or at least your part of the world) by doing things for people that they should do for themselves.

As mentioned in Chapter 6, even Moses fell for this deception. He was hand-picked by God to lead a nation of more than a million people. Yet he had to be confronted by an "outsider" to point out that he was not building disciples; he was trying to do way too much himself. It would not scale, even for Moses. This parable makes me feel a little better about what I'll share next.

Early in our work for clients, we tried to "help" them too much. We went beyond coaching to trying to make up for their lack of time and sometimes unwillingness to do what only they can do. I am surprised by how slow I was to see this. Especially since this is the model Jesus used from the beginning. He picked twelve people and focused on equipping them and "pushing" them to go out "two by two" to practice what they learned. Ultimately, he cut the cord and left the earth to emphasize that they had this responsibility. By leaving, He left no doubt as to their role.

The biblical model for helping people do what they should is to teach good principles and provide one-on-one and group accountability to support them but ultimately transfer ownership to mentees for their part of the plan. Mentoring is about reproducing leaders who take ownership.

If you want to build an organization that scales and continues to thrive over the long term, your leaders must consider themselves mentors.

If you want to build an organization that scales and continues to thrive over the long term, your leaders must consider themselves mentors or disciple-makers. In describing how followers of Christ should do this, the Bible says, "Therefore encourage one another and build one another up, just as you are doing" (1 Corinthians 5).

At this point you may be saying to yourself (hopefully), "Yes, it makes sense that I need to mentor others." But will you do it?

It seems crazy after forty years of life, to accept that we all struggle to do what we already know we should. No exceptions. The only thing crazier is to ignore this fact about ourselves and not do something about it. Ten years ago, our daughter realized this about my wife and me, and one Christmas she gave us ninety days of fitness coaching lessons. Ouch!

But ten years later, we have our Monday and Thursday "dates" with Greg, where we pay him to beat us into doing what we already know how to do but won't do without him. Part of Greg's value is that he shows us what to do, but by far the greater value is that he provides us the motivation and accountability to do it.

If you want to build a sustainable, healthy organization, you have to create this same dynamic in your workplace. Every leader has to be mentored *and* be a mentor. It is the only way the organization can sustain healthy growth.

And it is also the only way we weak humans get the ongoing encouragement we need to stay the course.

So how do you go about mentoring someone? The following are five tips that you can start using today.

Tip 1: Check Your Motives

I continue to beat the drum that motives matter most. It is through our teamwork that miracles come. And the only way we work together well is when relationships are right. For relationships to be right, motives (desires) have to be right.

In Chapter 7, I mentioned the apostle Paul's narrative about how to build a highly functioning Church. Following is an excerpt of one of his most quoted chapters.

And if I have prophetic powers, and understand all mysteries and all knowledge, and if I have all faith, so as to remove mountains, but have not love, I am nothing. If I give away all I have, and if I deliver up my body to be burned, but have not love, I gain nothing.

1 Corinthians 13

This passage was written to describe an essential truth for making the church work as designed. We are strong-willed people designed with great creative energy, and it is impossibly difficult to keep us on the same page. Paul is saying that only the agape type of love will do the job. And over the long haul, even churches fail at this. But it does not change the truth that, as leaders, caring for others is the first priority enabling our ability to lead.

> It does not change the truth that, as leaders, caring for others is the first priority enabling our ability to lead.

If you truly want to invest in building a difference maker, you need to start by asking yourself why you want to invest in someone else's life. Next you have to move from thought to action.

Tip 2: Commit to a Schedule

The problem with exploring motives is that they are hidden and can be faked. What can't be faked are our actions. If you are serious about mentoring your team, you need to commit to a schedule and stick to it.

> The problem with exploring motives is that they are hidden and can be faked. What can't be faked are our actions.

In Chapter 13, we described the necessity of creating a team development plan. This is a plan that shows how often you will meet with your people and for what purpose.

> "You are not important compared to everything else I have going on."

It encourages creating a training plan as well.

I remember one of my board members telling me that people spell love as "T I M E." This applies to our children, our spouses, and our team members. I have had hundreds of conversations with people who tell me their boss doesn't have time for them. Yes, they put something on the calendar, but the meetings are frequently missed, start late, and end early. In general their leader's actions shout loudly, "You are not important compared to everything else I have going on."

Tip 3: Do as I Do

> Teachers focus on "do as I say," but mentors focus on "do as I do."

Now we are confronted with the difference between teaching and mentoring. Teachers focus on "do as I say," but mentors focus on "do as I do." So the question becomes, How to spend your time? You must be clear about the behaviors and beliefs you want to build. In this case, you are developing leaders to serve in your organization as it grows. So you should mentor people to use the leadership model being used in the organization.

As a reminder, there are two dimensions to your mentoring: process skills and people skills (Figure 18.2).

You have one large advantage of mentoring someone at work: you can use a learn-by-doing approach. We all learn better when we can immediately apply what we are learning. By mentoring on the job and following the leadership development model of the organization, you have focused topics to mentor with and the advantage of immediate application, so learning is sped up.

But keep in mind that many times you will feel off track. The 2005 movie *World's Fastest Indian* is based on the true story of Burt Monroe, who set multiple speed records in the 1950s and 1960s with his remodeled Indian motorcycle. In one scene (Figure 18.3), Burt is looking out his windshield, trying, with all the strength he can muster, to keep his cycle on the black line painted on salt flats at

Sustainable Leadership Effectiveness

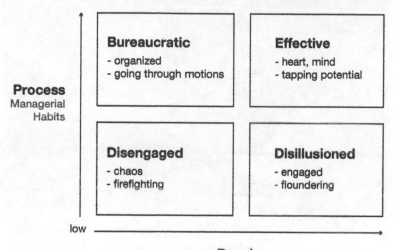

FIGURE 18.2 Mentoring process skills: sustainable leadership and effectiveness.
Source: LeadFirst.ai

Bonneville, Utah. The closer he can stay to the black line, the faster his time will be as he speeds between mile markers with timing devices.

His cycle is barely under control, and he is never on the line. He crosses back and forth over it by a few feet on either side as he focuses on it.

In this analogy, think of the line as representing a major purpose in your life. We are seldom on our line, but the line gives us something to adjust to as the surprises in life occur. Without the line, we live in chaos. We do not know whether to turn left or right at the next bump in the road.

Jesus used this approach all the time with His disciples. He was with them while He worked and

> Think of the line as representing a major purpose in your life. We are seldom on our line, but the line gives us something to adjust to as the surprises in life occur.

FIGURE 18.3 Scene from the *World's Fastest Indian*.
Source: 2929 Productions/Photo 12/Alamy Stock Photo.

constantly shared and interpreted what He was doing and why. Many times, they were off course. He expected that and course-corrected. And His approach was much more of a show by example than tell by lecture.

We can do the same. We can help those we are mentoring draw their line and show them how to get back on it by overcoming the chaos around them.

Tip 4: Transfer Ownership

The ultimate aim is to build enough maturity in the disciple so that they can stand on their own. They understand how to apply the lessons well enough to both use them effectively and to train someone else. That is the biblical standard of a disciple: training them until they can train someone else who trains someone else.

> That is the biblical standard of a disciple: training them until they can train someone else who trains someone else.

Most organizations are unwilling to pay the price to live up to this standard of replication. After two or three generations, the original model has become diluted and ineffective. A dilution in motives and methods is part of the reason organizations outgrow their own ability to execute.

Tip 5: Know Work Is Holy

Is leadership important? *Yes*—this is the whole premise of this book. You and everyone else were created to lead, to overcome, to win. You may lead yourself or teams of people, but regardless, everyone is influencing others.

To understand the importance of what you are doing, consider the meaning of the word *holy* in scripture. When God sets something aside for a purpose, He often declares it to be holy. There are many examples of pieces of furniture in the temple or other inanimate objects declared holy. People assigned to a specific role are dedicated to a purpose. Leaders and individual followers of Christ are referred to as holy.

> When God sets something aside for a purpose, He often declares it to be holy.

Living your life according to godly purposes is holy work. Building organizations that allow people to make a living and express their God-given talents is holy work. The distinction is that the term *holy* in the Bible is always used in the context of aligning with God's purposes.

Following is an illustration of how purpose, oneness, and holiness come together. Below are the instructions God gave for what the priests should wear in the time of Moses:

> *You shall speak to all the skillful, whom I have filled with a spirit of skill, that they make Aaron's garments to consecrate him for my priesthood.*
>
> *These are the garments that they shall make: a breast piece, an ephod, a robe, a coat of checker work, a turban, and a sash. They shall make holy garments for Aaron your brother and his sons to serve me as priests.*
>
> *Exodus 28*

Note in these instructions that a *purpose* is given (serve as priests). The thing to be produced is *one* thing (a garment) that is made of different pieces (breast-piece, ephod, a robe, a coat, a turban, and a sash), and the garment is referred to as "holy."

I explain this so that as we try to understand our work as leaders, we can use the parallels in the way God works to enlighten us. Although we are created in His image, we are limited in our understanding and certainly do not fully grasp God's purposes and holiness. Out of respect, I am careful not to abuse the term "holy."

So for the rest of us, the terms I use to show whether the pieces are working together properly are *good* and *bad* or *aligned* and *misaligned*. As with Monet (Chapter 4), part of our work as leaders is to decide whether our purposes are being fulfilled.

I can assure you from the authority of the Bible that leading yourself and leading others is holy work. It is why you exist. In my experience, when we pursue this holy work, we grow in our relationships with each other and God and experience the harmony and oneness that life was designed to be.

> I can assure from the authority of the Bible that leading yourself and leading others is holy work. It is why you exist.

Additional Wisdom about Mentoring

- "...what you have heard from me in the presence of many witnesses entrust to faithful men, who will be able to teach others also" (2 Timothy 2:2).
- "For I have given you an example, that you also should do just as I have done to you" (John 13:15).
- "Give instruction to a wise man, and he will be still wiser; teach a righteous man, and he will increase in learning" (Proverbs 9:9).
- "Whoever walks with the wise becomes wise, but the companion of fools will suffer harm" (Proverbs 13:20).

- "Let the wise hear and increase in learning, and the one who understands obtain guidance" (Proverbs 1:5).

- "Let no one despise you for your youth, but set the believers an example in speech, in conduct, in love, in faith, in purity" (1 Timothy 4:12).

- "The proverbs of Solomon, son of David, king of Israel: To know wisdom and instruction, to understand words of insight, to receive instruction in wise dealing, in righteousness, justice, and equity; to give prudence to the simple, knowledge and discretion to the youth—Let the wise hear and increase in learning, and the one who understands obtain guidance" (Proverbs 1:1–3).

- "Without counsel plans fail, but with many advisers they succeed" (Proverbs 15:22).

- "Know well the condition of your flocks, and give attention to your herds" (Proverbs 27:23).

- "What you have learned and received and heard and seen in me—practice these things, and the God of peace will be with you" (Philippians 4:9)

- "Oil and perfume make the heart glad, and the sweetness of a friend comes from his earnest counsel" (Proverbs 27:9).

- "Take my instruction instead of silver, and knowledge rather than choice gold, for wisdom is better than jewels, and all that you may desire cannot compare with her. I, wisdom, dwell with prudence, and I find knowledge and discretion" (Proverbs 8).

- "Let each of you look not only to his own interests, but also to the interests of others" (Philippians 2:4).

Epilogue

"Calling transforms life so that even the commonplace and menial are invested with the splendor of the ordinary."

Os Guinness, *The Call*

The quote above follows a story in *The Call* about a young Scottish woman, Jane D'Esterre, who was standing ready to jump to her death off a bridge. She was widowed suddenly by the death of her husband in a duel. Her despair was so great that caring for her two children did not outweigh the relief she sought.

> *As she stood on the stone bridge, she looked out and saw a young farmer plowing his field and whistling hymns as he worked.*
>
> *Meticulous, absorbed, skilled, he displayed such pride in his work that the newly turned furrows looked as finely executed as the paint strokes on an artist's canvas.*
>
> *Slowly she was drawn into the plowman's pride until admiration turned into wonder and wonder into rebuke. What was she doing collapsing into self-pity? How could she be so wrapped up in herself when two small children depended on her?*

Guinness relates that this woman was his great-great-grandmother. And that he would never have existed had it not been for the faithfulness of the farmer.

Life is challenging, even to the point of being overwhelming. We can relate to Jane standing on the bridge ready, thinking there were no better options. Hopefully, you see you were created with a special purpose—a design and a calling to overcome the chaos in your part of the world.

You have the desire and reason to shape your purposes in life, and you have the God-like ability to create the future you want to pursue in your imagination. And you have your strength and the strength of others to go with you on this journey.

As you go through life, pursuing your purpose, you lead yourself, and you lead others. *You may not have a title that says "manager," but know this. Leaders know where they are going, and just by living their lives, they influence those around them.*

Just as the young farmer did not know the influence he was having on Jane, the pursuit of his purpose with joy changed history. The Guinness family would not exist, and all the impact those people would have had would not exist.

Your life is God-given. It is important, and it is compounding in ways you will not understand until your time on this earth is completed. But faith says you can live today with the present reality that it is true.

You really are built to beat chaos!

Gary Harpst

Learning Resources

Following are some of my favorite learning resources and how they have influenced me on my journey.

From Peter Drucker's lifetime body of work, I learned the essence of leadership and management and by his example, lifelong learning.

From Michael Porter's many writings I learned what "strategy" really is.

From James Clear (*Atomic Habits*) I learned the significance of systems on habit sustainability.

From Patrick Lencioni (*5 Dysfunctions of a Team*) I learned the importance of sequencing values development in the right order.

From Os Guiness (*The Call*) I more deeply grasped the holiness of work.

From John Maxwell's life I see the integration of faith and work well integrated.

From Gregory Berns (*Iconoclast*) I learned the relationship of brain design and the deception of the law of large numbers.

From Ram Charan (many writings) I learned to think of execution as a discipline to be developed.

From Gregory Boyle (*Barking to the Choir*) I learned the power of focused caring.

From C.S. Lewis (*Mere Christianity*) I learned the significance of people wanting one thing but doing another.

From Stephen Covey (*Principle-Centered Leadership* and *The 7 Habits of Highly Effective People*) I learned how to help individuals be more effective and base business decisions on enduring principles.

From David Allen (*Getting Things Done*) I learned the power of managing personal chaos systematically.

From Michael Gerber (*The E Myth Revisited*) I learned about the confusion of roles all entrepreneurs go through as the business grows and how they must transition from working in the business to working on it.

From Robert Kaplan and David Norton (*The Balanced Scorecard, The Strategy-Focused Organization*) I learned the value of communicating strategy to all levels of the organization and getting organizations to develop the ability to focus on strategy execution as a core competence.

From Peter Senge (*The Fifth Discipline*) I learned the importance of approaching learning from a systems perspective.

From Jim Collins (*Built to Last, Good to Great*) I learned the importance of defining enduring values and living by them. I've grasped the power of focus and the difficulty of saying no.

From the Baldrige National Quality Program I learned a great deal about how to manage excellence systematically.

And finally, from the Bible I learned our purpose and how we are designed to fulfill that purpose.

Gordian™ Problem Solving App

For readers who would like to try the Gordian™ Problem Solving process described in Chapter 16 using the Gordian app, you can download it for free at the www.apple.com store or at the Android Play store at www.play.google.com.
Steps

1. Login to the store.
2. Search for Gordian™ Problem Solving (from LeadFirst.ai).
3. Enter the promo code "chaos".
4. Download.
5. Login to the app.
6. Follow the instructions in Chapter 16.

Have fun! Build teamwork.

- Get new approaches for tough problems.
- Get the quiet types sharing.
- Get the talkative ones listening.
- Get new perspectives on solutions.
- Prioritize where to start.

Gordian is owned and published by www.leadfirst.ai.

About the Author

Gary Harpst is the founder and CEO of LeadFirst.ai. LeadFirst was founded in 2001 (as Six Disciplines) with a mission of building effective leaders and helping small and mid-size companies manage change, grow, and execute. Its four-part leadership development system—composed of people skills, data-driven management skills, management platform, and just-in-time learning—helps organizations bring order out of this swirling chaos.

What makes LeadFirst's approach unique is that it connects *all* the dots. Some companies may focus on people and not systems or processes or vice versa. One without the other simply won't move the needle. In addition, its system-driven approach helps hardwire the habits, which is key to driving consistent, sustainable execution in a workplace that continues to evolve.

Formerly, Gary was a co-founder of and CEO of Solomon Software, which was acquired by Great Plains Software and soon sold to Microsoft. Gary has also co-founded Solomon Cloud Solutions and Beyond Software and serves as chairman of both companies.

Gary is a keynote speaker and insightful teacher who challenges and motivates his audiences. His passion is speaking about what effective leaders need to know, do, and be to overcome the chaos of everyday life. He unlocks biblical wisdom for unleashing the potential in every human being to lead themselves and others.

Gary's also been recognized as being one of the Top 100 of the nation's top thought leaders in management and leadership by *Leadership Excellence* magazine. He received an honorary doctorate from the University of Findlay. Gary speaks, interviews, teaches, and writes frequently on leadership, business, and the integration of faith at work. He has written three books: *Six Disciplines for Excellence*, *Execution Revolution*, and *Built to Beat Chaos* (Wiley).

Outside of his business interests Gary has served in secondary and higher education, nonprofit, and public service board positions and as an Elder and teacher in his church. He received a BS from The Ohio State University and an MBA from the Fisher School of Business (OSU).

He is enjoying marriage of thirty-seven years with his life partner Rhonda and their three children and four grandchildren.

Index